QUALITY ASSURANCE:
The Route to Efficiency and Competitiveness

ELLIS HORWOOD SERIES IN
APPLIED SCIENCE AND INDUSTRIAL TECHNOLOGY

Series Editor: Dr. D. H. SHARP, OBE, lately General Secretary, Society of Chemical Industry; formerly General Secretary, Insitution of Chemical Engineers; and former Technical Director, Confederation of British Industry

Published and in active publication

PRACTICAL USES OF DIAMONDS
A. BAKON, Research Centre of Geological Technique, Warsaw, and A. SZYMANSKI, Institute of Electronic Materials Technology, Warsaw
PREPARATION, PROPERTIES AND INDUSTRIAL APPLICATIONS OF ORGANOFLUORINE COMPOUNDS
Editor: R. E. BANKS, Department of Chemistry, University of Manchester, Institute of Science and Technology
POTTERY SCIENCE: Materials, Processes and Products
A. DINSDALE, lately Director of Research, British Ceramic Research Association
MATCHMAKING: Science, Technology and Manufacture
C. A. FINCH, Managing Director, Pentafin Associates, Chemical, Technical and Media Consultants, Stoke Mandeville, and S. RAMACHANDRAN, Senior Consultant, United Nations Industrial Development Organisation for the Match Industry
PAINT AND SURFACE COATING: Theory and Practice
Vol. 1: Colloid, Surface and Polymer Chemistry of Modern Surface Coatings
Vol. 2: Physical Properties of Liquid Coating Compositions and of Derived Films
Editor: R. LAMBOURNE, lately Section Manager, Research Department, ICI plc Paints Division
CROP PROTECTION CHEMICALS
B. G. LEVER, Development Manager, ICI plc Plant Protection Division
COMMERCIAL ASPECTS OF OILS AND FATS
R. J. F. LEYSEN, Market Manager, American Soybean Association, Belgium
HANDBOOK OF MATERIALS HANDLING
Translated by R. G. T. LINDKVIST, MTG, Translation Editor: R. ROBINSON, Editor, Materials Handling News. Technical Editor: G. LUNDESJO, Rolatruc Limited
FERTILIZER TECHNOLOGY
G. C. LOWRISON, lately of Fison's Fertilisers Ltd.
NON-WOVEN BONDED FABRICS
Editor: J. LUNENSCHLOSS, Institute of Textile Technology of the Rhenish-Westphalian Technical University, Aachen and W. ALBRECHT, Wuppertal
MICROCOMPUTERS IN THE PROCESS INDUSTRY
E. R. ROBINSON, Head of Chemical Engineering, North East London Polytechnic
QUALITY ASSURANCE: The Route to Efficiency and Competitiveness
L. STEBBING, Technical Director, Bywater Technology Limited
POLYMERS IN PACKING TECHNOLOGY
J. STEPEK, Czechoslovakia. Translation Editor: G. E. J. REYNOLDS, Surrey
REFRACTORIES TECHNOLOGY
C. STOREY, Consultant, Durham, one time General Manager, Refractories, British Steel Corporation
POLYSTYRENE AND ITS MODIFICATIONS
P. SVEC *et al.,* University of Chemical Technology, Prague
PETROLEUM TECHNOLOGY
A. H. SWEATMAN, Visiting Professor, Imperial College and G. A. HOGG, Natural Gas Consultant, lately of British Petroleum Company plc
PERFUMERY TECHNOLOGY 2nd Edition
F. V. WELLS, Consultant Perfumer and former Editor of Soap, Perfumery and Cosmetics, and M. BILLOT, former Chief Perfumer to Houbigant-Cheramy, Paris, Presidentd'Honneur de la Societe Technique des Parfumeurs de la France
THE MANUFACTURE OF SOAPS, OTHER DETERGENTS AND GLYCERINE
E. WOOLLAT, Consultant, lately of Unilever plc

QUALITY ASSURANCE:
The Route to Efficiency
and Competitiveness

LIONEL STEBBING, FIQA, FAQMC, SMASQC
Technical Director
Bywater Technology Limited
Hounslow, Middlesex

ELLIS HORWOOD LIMITED
Publishers · Chichester

Halsted Press: a division of
JOHN WILEY & SONS
New York · Chichester · Brisbane · Toronto

First published in 1986 by
ELLIS HORWOOD LIMITED
Market Cross House, Cooper Street,
Chichester, West Sussex, PO19 1EB, England
*The publisher's colophon is reproduced from James Gillison's drawing of the ancient Market
Cross, Chichester.*

Distributors:

Australia and New Zealand:
JACARANDA WILEY LIMITED
GPO Box 859, Brisbane, Queensland 4001, Australia

Canada:
JOHN WILEY & SONS CANADA LIMITED
22 Worcester Road, Rexdale, Ontario, Canada

Europe and Africa:
JOHN WILEY & SONS LIMITED
Baffins Lane, Chichester, West Sussex, England

North and South America and the rest of the world:
Halsted Press: a division of
JOHN WILEY & SONS
605 Third Avenue, New York, NY 10158, USA

© 1986 L. Stebbing/Ellis Horwood Limited

British Library Cataloguing in Publication Data
Stebbing, Lionel
  Quality assurance: the route to efficiency and competitiveness. —
(Ellis Horwood series in industrial technology)
1. Quality assurance
I. Title
658.5'68   TS156.6

ISBN 0–85312-944-4 (Ellis Horwood Limited)
ISBN 0–470–20298–X (Halsted Press)

Typeset in Times by Ellis Horwood Limited
Printed and bound in Great Britain by Butler & Tanner Ltd, Frome and London

Table of Contents

Foreword

by Mr John Butcher,
Parliamentary Under Secretary of State for Industry

It is not too long ago that the 'Made in Britain' label was recognized and respected throughout the world as a virtual guarantee of unmatched quality and performance.

Today of course we have things rather less our own way on world markets, even though our industry continues to produce its fair share of outstanding products.

That is partly a reflection of the enormous intensification of world competition during the last 30 years. Japan in particular has demonstrated that the route to economic success is the pursuit of ever higher standards of quality by continually setting new standards of technological innovation, reliability and performance which have made her the biggest exporter of manufactured goods in the world.

Certainly it has become increasingly clear that we will only increase our own share of domestic and world export markets by matching that level of commitment and competing on every aspect of quality to the point where 'Made in Britain' is once again synonymous with the very best the world can offer.

This book can contribute to helping British management to meet that challenge at a time when quality is increasingly the key to improved competitiveness. I hope it will be widely read. And because 1986 is Industry Year, which is also concerned with changing attitudes towards and within our industry, the publication of Mr Stebbing's book could scarcely be more timely.

Preface

It is unfortunate that quality assurance continues to be misunderstood and I have written this book to try to dispel some of the myths and break through the mystique surrounding the subject and to present what I believe to be the soundest philosophy. It is a consistent and logical approach which, if implemented and practised in everyday activities with total support from senior management, can lead only to 'getting it right first time — every time'.

I appreciate that some may not totally agree with my philosophies and methods but I have found that they do achieve the desired results; therefore some may have to alter their thinking radically to accept these philosophies and methods. There are many interpretations but I am convinced that this is the right one. If a change of thinking is required, I would refer you to that great statesman Sir Winston Churchill who said:

> There is nothing wrong in change if it is in the right direction. To improve is to change, so to be perfect is to have changed often.

Perfection is difficult to achieve but one can get very close to it with constant practise. Quality assurance is a skill and with any skill, once one has learned it, one must practise it to be perfect. There are many individuals who have helped me practise my skills and these same individuals have taught me much.

It would be impossible to list them all but some must be mentioned: David who did not believe me at first but who became my greatest convert; the two Alans and one Allan who made great contributions in many areas; Odvaar who taught me to understand the Norwegian approach; Eric and Bob who gave me the Canadian view; Willem whose persistence made me go into print and Yamanouchi san with whom I spent many delightful hours discussing the Japanese approach, not only with regard to the quality of the product but also regarding the quality of life.

No function can be said to be right unless it has been checked and confirmed, and without the assistance of Mike it would never have achieved its 'approved' status.

My wife Betty must receive the greatest appreciation. She painstakingly read and typed the final draft and gave me the encouragement and support that I needed when I felt I would never get it finished. Her remarks, after reading the final draft, were quite revealing: 'Very good but surely it is only common sense after all!'

Is it? I leave you, the reader, to decide.

Finally, my thanks must go to another David whom I regard as my frame-maker. I painted the picture and David framed it for me. He is my editor.

Lionel Stebbing
Rowledge
Surrey

Acknowledgements

The author wishes to acknowledge the assistance and co-operation of his colleagues at Bywater Technology Limited in permitting the free use of company material for adaptation within this book.

The author wishes also to acknowledge assistance with the supply of information from:

American Society of Mechanical Engineers, New York, NY 10017, USA
British Standards Institution, Certification and Assessment Department, Milton Keynes, Buckinghamshire MK14 6LE
Canadian Standards Association, Rexdale, Ontario, Canada M9W 1R3
Department of Trade and Industry, Standards and Quality Policy Unit, London SW1E 6RB
Institute of Quality Assurance, London SW7 2PG
National Society of Quality Circles, London SE1 2QZ

Introduction

THE TOTAL PRESENTATION

Richard Wagner (1813–1883), the great German composer, when he prepared his music dramas (operas), was at pains to bring together all the relationships between the different art forms involved in presenting a music drama. In so doing, and before committing himself to paper, he gave as much thought to the words, scenery, costume and overall presentation as to the music, his intention being to create a complete sound picture. Wagner gave this philosophy the title *Gesamtkunstwerk* (complete art work)—a bringing together of all activities and functions so that none is subservient to the other and that each is planned, controlled and executed in a formal and systematic manner. (This is one reason why Wagner's music dramas do not transfer well to the small screen as they should be seen as a whole to appreciate the total presentation).

Translated to the industrial scene, we would nowadays call this philosophy *quality assurance*. Perhaps the name is unfortunate as the word quality, in normal parlance, implies a subjective judgement. Quality, like beauty, is in the eye of the beholder. What is considered by one person to be of good quality, could be considered by another to be of poor quality, and vice versa. However, in the context of quality assurance, quality has a precise meaning. It is defined as:

> The totality of features and characteristics of a product or service that bear on its ability to satisfy a given need. (BS 4778—Glossary of terms used in quality assurance—including reliability and maintainability terms).

It is, therefore, necessary to understand the requirements of the customer and what he means by quality if the product or service is to satisfy the given need. In a consumer society the requirements of the customer can be identified only by market research, and information gained this way must be fed back to the finance, design and production departments for review for feasibility and implementation. In the case of major items, then the requirements must be identified by the customer in the form of detailed specifications.

In other words: What is the item required to do? What are its service requirements? What shape, size and colour are required? What is the expected service life and how is it to be disposed of when its usefulness has come to an end? The importance of the disposal of an item is often overlooked. Much will depend upon its size and complexity. In the case of small consumer items, disposal should be comparatively simple, but for capital plant consideration should be given at the outset to its ultimate decommissioning and dismantling. Hence the definition of quality referring to the totality of features and characteristics of a product or service.

ASSURANCE OF QUALITY

In order to assure quality, it is therefore necessary first to ensure that all the requirements for the total presentation are known. In other words, the customer's requirements must be sufficiently detailed to be fully understood by the supplier so that there are no areas of doubt as to the service requirements.

This is the *sine qua non* of any quality assurance scheme. The gathering together of all the information, the planning of all activities, and the detailing of precise instructions should all take place before any activity commences. Then the subsequent proper control of these activities becomes possible.

Quality assurance requires the total integration and control of all elements within a particular area of operation so that none is subservient to the other. These elements cover such aspects as administration, finance, sales, marketing, design, procurement, manufacture, installation, commissioning and even, as we have seen, decommissioning.

If all the elements of an operation are to be totally integrated so that none is subservient to the other, the role, or function, of each of these elements should first be established, and, as in Wagner's music dramas, there should be a director to bring it all together. Therefore, responsibility should be assigned for the establishment of requirements and the integration and control of all activities. Ultimately it is the senior executive of an organisation who must accept responsibility for this direction and for the quality of the items or services produced by his company.

Quality assurance is, therefore, a management function which cannot be delegated.

As will be shown, a properly constituted quality assurance department can produce a plan for action and a scheme to be followed but its implementation is a management responsibility.

Quality is not something that can be 'tacked on to' a manufacturing process: as we have seen, quality assurance is a philosophy of total integration of the business to achieve the required result.

Unfortunately, in all too many cases, this responsibility of management is not recognised and the central philosophy of quality assurance not appreciated. Attempts are all too often made by management to delegate the function to a department which is given a title containing the word quality, such as Quality Department, Quality Control Department, Quality

Assurance Department, or even a combination of all three, Quality Assurance/Quality Control Department. This latter title is usually abbreviated to QA/QC Department, which will be seen to be a total misnomer.

Quality assurance has thus become a very misconstrued and misunderstood concept due, at least in part, to its unfortunate title which is at best misleading and, at worst, meaningless, when one considers its total implications. Perhaps Wagner's portmanteau title *Gesamtkunstwerk* would be better. At least it pulls away from the word quality which, unless the precise definition (such as that of BS 4778) is known and appreciated—which it very rarely is—is the cause of much misunderstanding.

MYTHS AND MISCONCEPTIONS

It is important, before continuing further, to dispel some of the myths and misconceptions that surround quality assurance. The most popular misconceptions are that: it is very costly; it is a massive paper generator; and that it places emphasis on correcting deficiencies after the fact rather than preventing defects from occurring in the first place. It is necessary to consider also the proper role of the department which is given such an unfortunate title and which seems to indicate that it alone is responsible for quality.

It is important, in the first place, to understand what quality assurance is not.

It is not quality control or inspection.
It is not a super-checking activity.
It is not responsible for engineering decisions.
It is not a massive paper generator.
It is not a major cost area.
It is not a panacea for all ills.

Now perhaps an explanation is due to qualify all the above statements.

It is not quality control or inspection. Although a quality assurance programme will include quality control and inspection, both these activities form only a part of a company's total commitment to quality. They relate directly to the control of the manufactured item. These two activities have no involvement in activities which occurred upstream beforehand, such as design, procurement, sales and marketing. They should be considered, therefore, only as one of the elements in the total presentation.

It is not a super-checking activity. In other words, the Quality Assurance Department should not be responsible for checking everything done by others. For example, the Quality Assurance Department should not be responsible for checking engineering documents and specifications for engineering content or checking welding procedures for metallurgical content, but there are some quality assurance philosophies which do place the responsibility for these checking activities upon the Quality Assurance Department. This cannot be considered either efficient or cost-effective. The responsibility for such checks should be on those who are sufficiently qualified and experienced to determine the efficacy of the activity under review.

It is not responsible for engineering decisions. In other words the Quality Assurance Department should not have to make decisions regarding engineering activites. The only people who can be responsible for engineering decisions are engineers; that is what they are trained and qualified to do.

It is not a massive paper generator. However, because such things as mill certificates, test certificates and third party certification documents in general have become regarded as being necessary to meet quality assurance requirements, there is a misconception that all such paper is the necessary requirement of a quality assurance programme.

Mill certificates, test certificates, non-destructive testing certificates, etc., are requirements to satisfy conformance to specifications. Specifications are engineering documents, not quality assurance documents.

Unfortunately, in many organisations, quality control or inspection activities are the responsibility of the Quality Assurance Department and, consequently, the need for such documentation is seen as a quality assurance requirement rather than an engineering or production requirement.

Third party certification is also considered by many to be a quality assurance requirement. In the main third party certification is issued to identify that an item or service meets minimum requirements imposed by legislation. For example, safety and environmental standards which are rigidly imposed by government agencies on nuclear facilities and offshore drilling and production platforms are required to be certified by a regulatory body before commencement of operations. Such certification is a legislative requirement, not a quality assurance requirement.

However, a well-designed and fully implemented quality assurance programme will ensure and verify that the documentation and certification requirements are achieved in the most efficient manner. The responsibility for documentation and certification should not be placed on the Quality Assurance Department, as has often been done in the past. Hence the stigma of it being a massive paper generator and a major cost area. This leads nicely into the next statement.

It is not a major cost area. As far as documentation and certification are concerned, quality assurance is not a major cost area. There are procedural requirements to support a quality assurance programme but, having said that, any self-respecting organisation should have procedural controls in place in any event and should not have delayed their installation and implementation until the company has become so large and/or that control has been lost. It is a fact that many organisations have been in existence for many years before implementing quality assurance programmes. Initially, in these circumstances, the development and implementation of such programmes can be quite substantial but the cost should be equated against improvements in efficiency, productivity and profitability. The best time to implement a quality assurance programme is at the inception of a company. Prevention is better than cure.

It is not a panacea for all ills. Quality assurance will not cure everything but it will go a long way towards getting things right first time, every time.

We are all fallible creatures and we all make mistakes. The person who makes no mistakes makes nothing.

All activities, regardless of their nature, have some human input somewhere, sometime. The possibility of achieving perfection every time is, therefore, very remote but one should strive to achieve perfection most of the time. This can be achieved only by constant practise and continual updating of skills. The requirements for training to acquire new skills and to keep abreast of new technology, and for retraining where one has not participated in an activity for some time, will go a long way towards achieving perfection every time.

If quality assurance is none of those things then what is it?

WHAT IS QUALITY ASSURANCE?

It is cost-effective.
It is an aid to productivity.
It is a means of getting it right first time every time.
It is good management sense, and, most importantly:
It is the responsibility of everyone.

In the following chapters it is the intention to show how a well-developed, well-implemented and well-supported quality assurance programme can meet these five criteria of 'what quality assurance is' and to confirm that Wagner's *Gesamtkuntswerk* is, perhaps, a better title to describe the philosophy presently known as quality assurance.

1

The background to quality assurance

CUSTOMER—SUPPLIER RELATIONSHIP

The background to quality assurance is the customer–supplier relationship. The ultimate purpose of any quality assurance scheme is to ensure complete satisfaction by the customer with the goods or services provided by the supplier. This, in turn, implies an active rather than a passive relationship. The requirements of the customer must be determined in the first instance. Depending on the nature of the product or service, either the customer will, or should, provide a full specification of his requirements, or the supplier, by market research and feedback from the market-place, will produce goods to a presumed customer requirement. Any quality assurance scheme must, therefore, involve the customer, either directly or indirectly. Although this customer–supplier relationship may be regarded, at least partly, as external to the supplier's activities, much the same philosophy applies internally within a supplier's work-place, at each stage of design through to manufacture. The customer may be regarded as the next stage in the process and so a quality assurance scheme applies throughout the whole complex of activities—*Gesamtkunstwerk*, as outlined in the Introduction.

Often in the past, the quality level of an item was defined more by the experience of a supplier than by any specific requirements of a customer. The customer stated his need in broad terms and the supplier manufactured an item which he considered filled that need. It was only when the item was complete that it was determined whether or not it suited the customer's requirements.

Although that was many years ago, these practices did, to a certain extent, spill over into modern industry, the only improvements being that very basic objectives were conveyed verbally or framed into very sketchy fabrication procedures.

The inspector, who usually worked for and reported to, the production department, had little idea of the full inspections required as insufficient data were given, due to inadequate information from the customer and lack of interface with the design or engineering department.

Many inspection results were accepted by the customer purely on the basis of his confidence in the manufacturer. However, the customer sometimes gave himself a little added assurance by having a representative at the manufacturer's works to witness some of the inspection and test points.

Sometimes defects were not discovered until manufacture was at an advanced stage, often leading to costly repair work, and sometimes involving scrapping, with the inevitable schedule delays. In spite of frequent inspection, not all defects were detected and this resulted in the in-service failures with which we are all too familiar.

This was the system (or lack of system) largely practised until very recently, and it is not surprising that customers often criticised the poor quality and delivery performance of their suppliers. This approach has seriously affected the ability to be competitive in overseas markets.

THE SYSTEMATIC APPROACH

During recent years with design, manufacture and installation processes becoming increasingly complex and safety and environmental requirements becoming more stringent, the old inspection practices have been found to leave too many areas open to human error, notwithstanding the quality and extent of inspection coverage.

Unfortunately, there is still the tendency to cling to these old inspection practices, which serve only to identify that an item or service is acceptable or unacceptable on a 'go/no-go' basis. Instead, one should now be looking at methods which reduce the amount of inspection and non-destructive testing activities. Everyone in an organisation should be responsible for the quality of the work they produce rather than relying on the activities of inspectors subsequently to discover any faults.

The results of these old inspection practices leave much to be desired.

The philosophy now is to insist on objective or real evidence of quality rather than make an assumption by inspection, or accept a guarantee by a contractor or supplier, that the required quality does exist.

This real evidence of quality must be seen to exist, not only in the completed item but in all activities which are involved in completing that item: design, procurement, manufacture and installation. By controlling all those functions in a systematic manner one can be reasonably assured that each activity is right before the next activity commences.

However, the evidence of quality discussed so far relates to all the activities concerned with the actual design, procurement, manufacture and installation of an item. These activities in themselves, if they are under control, will give the customer the item in a 'fit for purpose' condition and within budget and on schedule. There are many other functions outside these areas which indirectly affect the efficiency of achieving fitness for purpose. These include such functions as: market research, sales, finance, administration and maintenance, and should all be included in the total quality assurance programme. Thus we would not only achieve fitness for purpose but it would be achieved in the most efficient and cost-effective manner.

Inevitably such increase in efficiency must lead to increased profitability with all its attendant benefits.

REAL OR OBJECTIVE EVIDENCE OF QUALITY

This is the evidence which confirms that all activities within each of the functions of design, procurement, manufacture and, in the case of large projects, site construction and commissioning, have been carried out in accordance with established working methods. These methods are identified in documents, which are known as *procedures.*

Procedures will detail the purpose and scope of an activity and will also identify how, when, where and by whom the activity is to be carried out.

Emanating from such activities will be documents which will detail the results of activities or tests. A design activity, for example, will produce a document such as a specification, a drawing or a data sheet. A procurement activity will produce a document such as a tender package, purchase order or contract. An inspection or test activity will produce a document such as a mill certificate, non-destructive testing certificate or heat treatment certificate.

THE NEED FOR AUDIT

It is these procedures, together with the documentation, which give the objective evidence of quality.

Having then established procedures to cover all activities and functions of a company, how can it be ensured that all these procedures are being properly adhered to? What takes the place of inspection in the old system of operation? The answer is a compliance audit.

What is an audit expected to prove?

An audit is undertaken to indicate whether a procedure, or system, is working satisfactorily. It readily highlights non-conformances and should lead to action being taken to correct them and prevent their recurrence.

The requirement for quality assurance audits are determined by management and, as such, management responsibilities should be integrated into the quality assurance programme.

Therefore, it is a management decision to implement audits and, in order for an audit to work effectively, the group concerned with implementing audits must have the organisational freedom to oversee the development, implementation and maintenance of the quality programme. In this context the word 'group' can imply as few as one or even a part-time activity, depending on the size and nature of the company.

As has already been stated, for the sake of convenience, this group is usually given the title 'quality assurance department'. This is perhaps unfortunate because, as we have seen, quality assurance is a philosophy which should be practised throughout an entire organisation and should not be regarded as the responsibility of just one department.

To secure the required authority, organisational freedom and independence, it is therefore essential for the quality assurance manager to report direct to senior management. This is a *sine qua non* of any effective quality assurance scheme. Any attempt to place the so-called Quality Assurance Department within, say, the Production Department, indicates that the management has not appreciated the philosophy of quality assurance.

Experience has shown that in most cases where quality assurance has been ineffective, this has been largely due to an incorrect 'chain of command'. The organisation for quality will be covered in greater detail in Chapter 5.

THE NEED FOR PROCEDURES

It follows that in order to assess and report any procedural non-conformancies within any discipline or department, and to obtain positive corrective action, it is imperative that all personnel within the Quality Assurance Department are adequately qualified and experienced and are accepted and respected as such. The Department should not be regarded as a policeman but as a guide, philosopher and friend!

To implement a quality assurance programme and to assess and report shortcomings within the programme, the Quality Assurance Department must have bases upon which to work. These bases are the written procedures which were identified earlier. These procedures should detail 'what' is required or is to be controlled; 'who' is responsible for ensuring the requirement is met, or the control carried out; and 'how', 'when', 'where' and possibly 'why' it is controlled. In addition, the procedures will describe how quality and safety requirements will be accounted for.

As well as taking account of quality and safety requirements, it is also important that procedures indicate how interface problems between departments or disciplines can be avoided. The procedures which involve an interface between departments or disciplines must, therefore, have the approval of all those groups directly concerned. A procedure should be written by the main discipline or department concerned, in consultation with the quality assurance department, to ensure that all relevant quality and safety requirements are included and that the document is capable of being audited.

The methods and techniques of auditing will be dealt with in greater detail in Chapter 15.

2

Principles, philosophies, standards and procedures

In a complex field such as quality assurance, full codification in the form of national standards or codes of practice is virtually impossible. Various aspects of the discipline have, however, been so covered. As mentioned in the Introduction, the definition of quality as used throughout this book is that of BS 4778. Other national standards and codes of practice have been produced, mainly to give guidance on quality programmes and their levels of intensity.

THE QUALITY PROGRAMME LEVEL

When reference is made to a particular quality level, in many instances this refers to sampling inspection percentages. However, the reference to a quality programme level carries an entirely different meaning.

In the main, quality programme standards are issued in Levels, usually three in number, as follows:

Level 1 covering design, manufacture and installation.
Level 2 covering manufacture and installation.
Level 3 covering final inspection and/or test.

There are, as with most things, exceptions to the rule. The nuclear industry, for example, has only one level, which is equivalent to Level 1 described above, whereas the Canadian Standard Z299 has four levels, but in all cases Level 1 includes activities and functions relating to design, manufacture and installation.

There are two types of quality assurance standards: industry-related standards and general standards.

Industry-related standards are those developed by purchasing bodies to enable suppliers to meet the quality requirements of a particular industry. These are normally produced as an aid to government procurement or in industries where there is an important and overriding safety requirement.

Examples include defence, aerospace and nuclear industries.

General standards are those issued by national bodies to give guidance to industry in general on quality assurance programme development. They are normally for guidance purposes only.

Regardless of the country of origin or the industry connotations, the differences within these standards are, in the main, quite small. Unfortunately, as is the case with quality, there are semantic problems, particularly in the use of the terms *system* and *programme*. There is, unfortunately, no consistency in this. It would be easier if it could be said that the British Standards use *system* and all others *programme* but this is not the case. BS 5750 (British) carries the general title Quality *Systems* whereas BS 5882 (also British) is identified with a title which includes the words quality assurance *programme*. However, as the majority of the standards use the term *programme* it is this word which will be used throughout this book to describe the integration and effective execution of all management, design and manufacturing activities.

Reverting back to the Wagnerian philosophy of *Gesamtkunstwerk* then the programme would be equivalent to the complete score, together with scenario and costume details. Following on from that, one could identify a system as being an act and a procedure as a scene. When mention is made later to a manual, this could be related to the overture. By drawing away from the word quality, these descriptions should enable one to relate the applicable term more readily to its function.

COMPARISON OF QUALITY ASSURANCE STANDARDS

Figure 2.1 identifies a number of the standards which address the criteria applicable to quality assurance programmes. Each standard is unique in its own way, yet, if the contents of each are evaluated, common factors are found.

A basic list of 25 functions, which could be considered to represent the typical criteria for a Level 1 quality assurance programme, has been used as a norm and from it a comparison table compiled (see Fig. 2.2). Each of the numbers beneath the standards refer to the applicable section of that standard. This table does indicate common ground with regard to procedural requirements, but what it does not identify are the areas of *emphasis*. For example, BS 5882 and ANSI/ASME NQA.1 place much more emphasis on design control than do the other standards. Both BS 5882 and NQA.1 are quality assurance programmes relating to nuclear power plant projects. The other standards place their emphasis more on manufacturing.

Many major projects (such as an offshore platform or petrochemical plant) have a large design content and require design controls just as much as does the nuclear industry; therefore one must extract the design elements from the nuclear standards.

On the other hand, with the remaining elements of a project, namely procurement, manufacture, installation and commissioning, the requirements can be adequately covered by using such standards as BS 5750 or

Typical quality assurance standards

UK
BS 5750 Quality Systems.
Part 1—Specification for design, manufacture and installation. (Guidance notes—Part 4).
Part 2—Specification for manufacture and installation. (Guidance notes—Part 5).
Part 3—Specification for final inspection and test. (Guidance notes—Part 6).

BS 5882 Specification for a total quality assurance programme for nuclear power plants.

DEF STAN 05-21/1 Quality control system Requirements for Industry.
05-24/1 Inspection Requirements for Industry.
05-29/1 Basic Inspection Requirements for Industry.

NORWAY
NS 5801 Requirements for the contractor's quality assurance. Quality assurance system.
NS 5802 Requirements for the contractor's quality assurance. Inspection system.
NS 5803 Requirements for the contractor's quality assurance. Basic inspection.

CANADA*
CSA Z299.1 Quality Assurance Program Requirements.
CSA Z299.2 Quality Control Program Requirements.
CSA Z299.3 Quality Verification Program Requirements.
CSA Z299.4 Inspection Program Requirements.

USA
ANSI/ASME NQA-1 Quality Assurance Program Requirements for Nuclear Facilities.

*NB. Revised August 1985. Now CAN3–Z299 Categories 1, 2, 3 & 4.

Fig. 2.1 — Typical quality assurance standards.

Quality assurance standards — comparison table

		NS5801	BS5750:1	05-21/1	Z299.1*	BS5882*	NQA-1*
1.	Quality programme	1	4.1	201	3.1	1	II.2
2.	Organisation	2	4.2	202	3.2	2	II.1
3.	Audits	16	4.3	104	3.3	18	II.18
4.	Quality programme documents	1	4.1	NSI	3.4	1	II.2
	—Manual	1	NSI	NSI	3.4.1	1	II.2
	—Inspection and test plans	1	NSI	NSI	3.4.2	11	II.11
5.	Manufacturing control	10	4.12	211	3.5.12	9	II.9
6.	Planning (contract review)	3	4.4	203	3.5.1	1	II.2
7.	Design control	6	4.8	207	3.5.2	3	II.3
8.	Documentation and change control	5	4.9	208	3.5.3	4&6†	II.4&6†
9.	Control of inspection, measuring and test equipment	9	4.10	209	3.5.4	12	II.12
10.	Control of purchased materiel and services	7	4.11	210	3.5.5	7	II.7
11.	Incoming inspection	7	4.11	210	3.5.6	10	II.10
12.	Purchaser-supplied materiel (Free issue)	NSI	4.13	212	3.5.17	NSI	NSI
13.	In-process inspection	10	4.12	211	3.5.7	10	II.10
14.	Final inspection	15	4.14	213	3.5.8	10	II.10
15.	Sampling	NSI	4.15	214	3.4.2	10	II.10
16.	Inspection status	11	4.17	216	3.5.9	14	II.14
17.	Identification and traceability	8‡	4.12‡	NSI	3.5.10	8‡	II.8‡
18.	Handling and storage	8	4.18	217	3.5.11	13	II.13
19.	Work instructions	4	4.5	204	3.4.3	5	II.5
20.	Special processes	10	4.12	211	3.5.13	9	II.9
21.	Preservation, packaging and shipping	8	4.18	217	3.5.14	13	II.13
22.	Records	12	4.6	205	3.5.15	17	II.17
23.	Non-conformances	13	4.16	215	3.5.16	15	II.15
24.	Corrective action	14	4.7	206	3.5.18	16	II.16
25.	Training	NSI	4.19	NSI	3.3	2	II.2

*Identifes criticality and quality programme level evaluation.
†Change control covered under design control.
‡Traceability not separately identified.
NSI=Not separately identified.

Fig. 2.2 — Quality assurance standards—comparison table.

CSA Z299 as a basis.

From this it will be seen that no single standard fits any industry completely; therefore, it is necessary to adapt what is already available. The word *adapt* is used with great emphasis. When buying a suit 'off the peg', unless one is of average build it never fits properly and will need to be adjusted in the right places. Similarly, no industries are 'of average build'; they are all unique in their quality assurance requirements and, therefore, existing standards need tailoring.

INDUSTRY COMPARISONS

Figures 2.3, 2.4 and 2.5 show comparisons between offshore, nuclear and

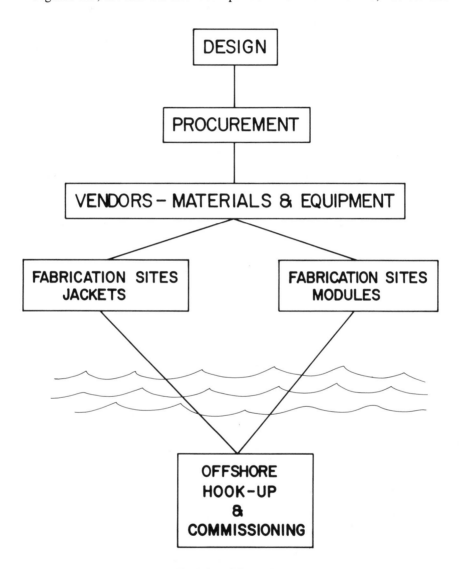

Fig. 2.3 — Offshore industry.

aerospace projects. One vital area which does not apply in the nuclear and aerospace projects, and is unique to an offshore project, is the fabrication site. By the time a module or jacket leaves the fabrication site it has got to be right. If it is not 'right' and faults are discovered when installed offshore, quite apart from losses due to schedule delays and production shortfalls, repairs offshore can cost fifteen times as much as onshore repairs.

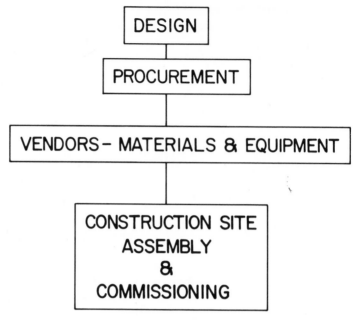

Fig. 2.4 — Nuclear industry.

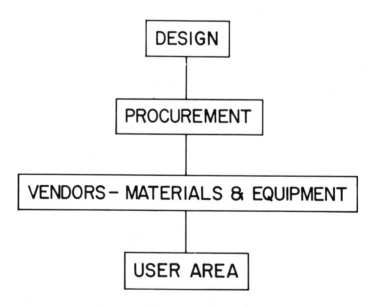

Fig. 2.5 — Military/aerospace industries.

Although fabrication sites, in the main, utilise purchaser-supplied materials and equipment, they require in-house controls just as much as a manufacturer but with a different emphasis—more towards receiving inspection, special processes, traceability, and the like. As an example, Fig. 2.6 gives an indication of differing procedural requirements throughout a major project.

PROCEDURES

In the background to quality assurance (Chapter 1) reference was made to a procedure. It is now worthwhile to look briefly into the preparation of a procedure.

Format

All procedures, to be effective, should be consistent in their presentation. As with any type of document, uniformity of presentation is of paramount importance; therefore guidelines should be formulated for the preparation of procedures. In other words, there should be a *procedure for writing procedures*. All procedures should carry the same contents list, although the number of sections within a procedure may differ from company to company, according to requirements, but as a minimum there should be three sections, i.e. 'Purpose and Scope', 'Procedure' and 'Documentation'. The development of the procedure is dealt with in detail in Chapter 9.

Procedure-writing responsibilities

The need for a procedure has to be identified by a responsible person within an organisation. Usually, when formulating a quality assurance programme, this need will be determined by senior management, taking into account the activities of the organisation concerned. The establishment and implementation of procedures can be undertaken only by personnel who are familiar with the activities and functions to be controlled. Unfortunately, in practice, the quality assurance department tends to be given the sole responsibility for procedure writing, whereas it could be said that the only procedures which can be effectively written by the quality assurance department are those relating to auditing, corrective action and auditor qualification and training. The proper practice is for the quality assurance department to be instrumental in recommending procedural requirements in consultation with the department or discipline concerned.

Once the procedural subject has been determined, and an author delegated to carry out the work, the procedure should be written utilising the agreed format.

QUALITY ASSURANCE MANUAL, PROGRAMME AND PLAN

Before a quality assurance programme can be established, there must be agreement on what that programme is intended to achieve. It can be seen from Fig. 2.6 that a design contractor places a different emphasis on certain

Procedural requirement through the project phases

	Design	Procurement	Manufacture	Installation and Commissioning	Operation and Maintenance	Decommissioning
1. Quality programme	0	0	0	0	0	0
2. Organisation	0	0	0	0	0	0
3. Audits	0	0	0	0	0	0
4. Quality programme documents	0	0	0	0	0	0
—Manual	—	—	0	—	—	—
—Inspection and test plans	—	—	0	0	0	0
5. Manufacturing control	0	0	0	0	0	0
6. Planning	0	0	0	—	—	—
7. Design control	0	—	*	—	—	—
8. Documentation and change control	0	0	0	0	0	0
9. Control of inspection, measuring and test equipment	—	—	0	0	0	0
10. Control of purchased materiel and services	—	0	0	*	*	—
11. Incoming inspection	—	—	0	*	*	—
12. Purchaser-supplied materiel	—	—	0	*	—	—
13. In-process inspection	—	—	0	0	—	—
14. Final inspection	—	—	*	0	0	0
15. Sampling	—	—	0	—	—	—
16. Inspection status	0	—	0	0	0	0
17. Identification and traceability	—	—	0	0	0	0
18. Handling and storage	0	0	0	0	0	0
19. Work instructions	0	0	0	0	0	0
20. Special processes	—	—	0	0	0	0
21. Preservation, packaging and shipping	—	—	0	0	0	*
22. Records	0	0	0	0	0	0
23. Non-conformances	0	0	0	0	0	0
24. Corrective action	0	0	0	0	0	0
25. Training	0	0	0	0	0	0

0 = Requirement.
* = Requirement in some cases.
— = No requirement.

Fig. 2.6 — Procedural requirements through the project phases.

in-house controls than does, say, the fabrication site mentioned earlier. Therefore a company's requirements, together with all regulatory requirements, should be established and documented.

At this stage it is worthwhile identifying the differences between a manual, programme and plan. Fig. 2.7 identifies by diagrammatic means

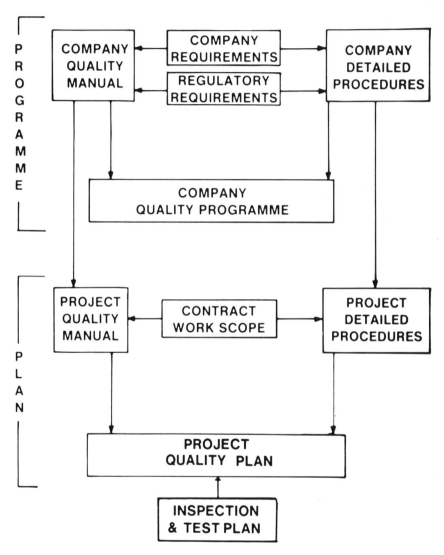

Fig. 2.7 — Programme/plan.

those differences but these will be dealt with in greater detail in Chapter 10.

Quality manual

BS 4778 defines a quality manual as 'a document setting out the general quality policies, procedures and practices of an organisation'.

The word 'general' is important in this definition. A quality manual is usually the first indication a prospective customer receives of a company's approach to quality assurance. This document should set out the company's intentions. It should contain as a minimum: a policy statement; authority and responsibilities; organisation; system outlines; and a procedures index. It should not, however, contain detailed procedures. Not only would their insertion make the document a very costly item but updating would be a continual problem. Procedures can be amended without affecting the outline in the manual and should be made available at the point of use. The actual development of the quality manual is described in Chapter 8.

Quality programme

This is defined in BS 4778 as 'a documented set of activities, resources and events serving to implement the quality system of an organisation'.

We have seen that the manual describes the intent, i.e. what is to be done. The procedures detail not only what but who, how, when, where and possibly why. Thus, the manual plus the supporting detailed procedures comprise the company's quality programme.

Quality plan

Again referring to BS 4778, a quality plan is defined as 'a document derived from the quality programme (extended if necessary) setting out the specific quality practices, resources and activities relevant to a particular contract or project'.

When the company's quality programme is applied to a given project or contract there is invariably the requirement for some form of adjustment or modification to suit that particular project or contract work scope. This adjustment or modification can take the form of either additions to, or reductions in, the corporate programme.

For example, a contractor who can have an involvement in all activities from design through to installation has to develop a programme to cover all these functions. This contractor, however, may win a contract for design only, in which case he will extract only those procedures relating to design and 'front' them with a manual unique to that contract. This manual plus the supporting procedures becomes the project quality plan (see Chapter 9).

In essence, that is how it should be but one still encounters plans being referred to as programmes and vice versa, with even instances of a document being entitled 'Quality assurance programme/plan'.

Project quality plan

Before leaving this subject, we need to touch briefly on who defines project quality policy. There are a number of ways a customer can set up his project management team (PMT), for example:

Customer PMT—where the customer will actually manage the project utilising his own staff and resources.

Integrated PMT—where the customer, together with a main contractor, will manage the project, utilising staff and resources from both areas. In other words, pooling resources and assigning the best person to a given job.

Contractor PMT—where a contractor is given the responsibility for managing the project.

Detail design contractor with project management responsibilities—where a contractor is engaged to undertake the design of a given plant or structure and will manage the procurement, manufacture and installation.

In the case of customer PMT, the project quality requirements will be established by the customer and imposed upon all main contractors who will, in turn, develop their own quality plan in accordance with their scope of work.

In the case of an integrated PMT, the project quality requirements will be established by the customer/contractor but in all probability the emphasis will be based upon customer philosophies. Again, the main contractors will be expected to develop their own quality plans in accordance with those requirements related to their scope of work.

Where a contractor is employed to manage a project, the quality requirements will be identified by the customer and the contractor will develop a project plan which will be reviewed and probably approved or agreed with by client, prior to imposing it on all subcontractors.

Similarly, where a detail design contractor has been engaged not only to undertake the design but also to manage the project, then this design contractor will develop the project plan and impose it on all subcontractors.

3

The penalties of inadequate procedures

THE REINVENTION OF THE WHEEL

Experience has shown that, all too often, the simple failure to learn from past mistakes and to profit from expensively acquired experience can lead to inefficient operation and expensive reworking—particularly in industries engaged in project work. In the absence of a proper corporate quality assurance programme each new project becomes a 'one-off', leading in popular parlance to the 'reinvention of the wheel'.

Invariably at the start of any new project or contract one goes through the agonising activity of developing and implementing project or contract procedures. In the absence of a corporate programme this activity starts from scratch without being able to identify problem areas which have been encountered previously. Communication is partly to blame for this but, in the main, the problem lies in the absence of a uniform system of working which is regularly reviewed, has senior management support and which is utilised on every contract.

The results of this 'reinvention of the wheel' soon become apparent. The start of a project or contract is usually the most unproductive, inefficient and unprofitable period and the same problems manifest themselves later on.

Experience has shown that the following statements and questions are frequently made or asked:

'Why didn't you specify ... ?'
'Who approved it?'
'Why wasn't I included in the distribution?'
'Who authorised that change?'
'Where is the documentation?'
'I can't read it!'
'That is not my responsibility!'
'Why did we buy from those people?'
'Who inspected that?'
'I didn't have an up-to-date specification!'
'We never had time!'

'But we have always done it that way!'

All of these need never have been said. Let us take each in turn.

Why didn't you specify ... ?

This is a question often asked during the later stages of a project or contract when the material and/or equipment received is incompatible with service requirements.

A typical example is equipment intended for sour-service use being received only to be found later to be unsuitable for such service. The consequences of this are:

— Equipment to be reordered to the correct specification.
— Additional cost.
— Schedule delays.

This situation has arisen because either one, two or all of three things occurred:

(a) Service conditions were not known at time of specification development.
(b) The specification was either not checked or not checked properly by competent personnel.
(c) The design engineer was not sufficiently knowledgeable or experienced.

In condition (a), the service requirements should have been identified at project start-up or as soon as possible thereafter.

Remedy—develop and implement contract review or design criteria review procedure at early design stage, so that all are aware of the details of the contract work scope.

In condition (b), the specification should have been checked by appropriately qualified and experienced personnel using approved checklists.

Remedy—develop and implement a design validation procedure during design stage, which will identify who is responsible for checking the appropriate documents.

In condition (c), the design engineer should have been suitably qualified and experienced.

Remedy—develop sufficiently detailed job specifications and implement in-house training schemes to cover any shortfalls in an employee's experience.

Who approved it?

One of three things has possibly happened here:

(a) There is no approval signature.
(b) The signatory is unknown and possibly unauthorised.
(c) Signature is not legible.

Each condition should have been identified during the design stage.

Remedy—develop and implement a design document approval register, with sample signatures, at project start-up. This should be a fundamental requirement of any document validation procedure and should be identified and established during the early stages of a company's establishment or project start. Those responsible for approving documents should have their signatures registered, as is required, for example, in banking, in which registered signatures are required to prevent unauthorised individuals drawing from the account. A document validation approval register will act in a similar manner.

Why wasn't I included in the distribution?
This question could be countered with the question: 'Should you have been included in the distribution?' Too many times distribution lists are developed which include personnel who have no involvement in the activity. If, however, the answer is yes then the document distribution procedure is either non-existent or is not being adhered to.
  Remedy—develop and implement a document distribution list which will form part of the document control procedure.
  Keep document distribution to an absolute minimum.
  All distribution lists should be developed from the 'need to know' rather than the 'want to know' situation. We all like to see our name in print, it makes one feel important, but do we really have an input into the document? It should be a management responsibility to formulate distribution lists and these should be compiled as early as possible.

Who authorised that change?
This goes hand in hand with 'Who approved it?' Changes to documents should receive the same attention as the original documents.
  Remedy—develop and implement a document change control procedure which will interface with the validation procedure.

Where is the documentation?
Material or equipment has been received without the supporting documentation (test results, material analysis, and the like). What happens now? The material/equipment has to be quarantined pending receipt of documentation, thus taking up storage space and possibly delaying construction. This situation has probably been caused by the supplier/manufacturer not having completed the documentation at time of inspection, or shipment, but being instructed probably by unauthorised personnel to ship the material/equipment and send on the documentation later.
  This is short-sighted policy as it can cause only delay and frustration and may lead to incorrect material being released for use.
  As material/equipment received without documentation cannot be used until the documentation is received, the supplier should accept responsibility for storage as the shipment is not complete without the necessary documentation. The contract on the supplier should make this clear.
  Remedy—ensure in procurement packages the requirement for documentation to form an integral part of the contract. Also instruct inspection

personnel not to release any items without the specified documentation, and then support that instruction to the full.

I can't read it!

Obviously an illegible copy of a document which has found its way into project records. This again results in frustration and delay.

Unauthorised copying of documents may be the cause here. This is a common problem, as it is so much easier to borrow a document and copy it oneself rather than go through the procedure of obtaining an authorised copy.

Remedy—set up and implement a strict document control system which identifies responsibility for document reproduction. This system to specify method of document reproduction; identification of documents; authority and approval.

An officially reproduced document can be identified with the words 'official copy' using red ink (or such other colour which will not reproduce in its original colour). Any document not carrying such identification should be regarded as unofficial and treated accordingly.

That is not my responsibility!

A very good excuse and in many instances perfectly valid. A well-written job specification will identify a person's responsibilities and reporting routes.

In too many cases a job specification states in great detail the major responsibilities relevant to the position, only to be invalidated by an appended statement such as 'and other responsibilities which may from time to time be delegated by your supervisor'.

This is an 'escape clause'.

Remedy—make job specifications clear and concise. When responsibilities are assigned over and above those indicated, then an amendment should be made to the job specification in writing. This is a safeguard, not only to the employee but also to the supervisor.

Why did we buy from those people?

Perhaps the recipient of the material or equipment knows something about the supplier which has not been communicated to the purchasing body. This statement would be made only if there has been some bad experience with the company concerned.

When assessing a possible supplier (a subject which will be dealt with later) all information should be made available.

Remedy—ensure that procedures take into account previous performance in vendor assessment. This means there must be a system to update vendor records with information from project or contract groups.

Who inspected that?

The inspector gets the blame in this case, but was it really his fault? Obviously an item has been received which is not considered by the recipient to be acceptable. Does the recipient have the correct information to make such a judgement? Perhaps the specification was wrong or perhaps the item was released without being controlled. There are many possibilities. Do not be too quick to pass judgement. It is very easy to blame the inspector . . . or the night shift!

This leads naturally into the next statement.

I didn't have an up-to-date specification!

Those who work, or have worked, in an inspection environment will have some sympathy with anyone who has to make such a statement. One cannot always blame the inspector for not having up-to-date documentation. Many are often instructed to inspect an item against a specification to be made available to them by the vendor. Therefore, one is reliant upon the vendor to supply all up-to-date information, but one really does not know whether it is up to date or not. This is a difficult situation to be in!

Also, the inspector can be given very sketchy information in the form of a telex, letter or telephone message, from which he may be expected to carry out a responsible inspection. If he complains he may be reprimanded for nit-picking.

Remedy—verify that the inspector is supplied with sufficient up-to-date information to carry out his inspection properly. This will be influenced by an effective and well-implemented document control procedure.

The inspector should be given the responsibility to determine for himself whether he has sufficient, and up-to-date, information to carry out his task. If he suspects shortcomings, then he should be supported in delaying the inspection until sufficient and correct information is received.

A personal experience is given to illustrate the point. During his early days in industry, the author was called upon to carry out an inspection assignment on equipment with which he was not completely familiar. It was a case of obeying orders as the job description included the 'escape clause' referred to above.

The equipment in question was for a hospital in Mexico and, the author having recently returned to work after undergoing an appendectomy, his supervisor considered he had the most recent applicable experience.

He was instructed to obtain all relevant information from the supplier — which he did.

The inspection was duly completed and the equipment released for shipment, only to be rejected upon arrival at the hospital in Mexico. The question asked was inevitable: 'Who inspected that?'

Naturally a very searching examination was held to determine what had gone wrong.

The information given by the supplier was, as far as he was concerned, correct. He had supplied the equipment in accordance with the purchase order and the inspection confirmed this. However, the investigation showed that the information given in the purchase order was incomplete. The equipment should have been supplied to an earlier catalogue reference description so as to interface with the equipment already installed at the hospital. The supplier had provided the latest type, which was not what was required, but had in effect been ordered.

In this instance, it was not a case of an up-to-date specification not being available but of the correct specification not having been used.

This incident led to an analysis of what had gone wrong and what should be done to prevent a recurrence of the situation. Evidently there was a lack of information in the contract documents, probably brought about by insufficient liaison with the engineering function and no independent check had been carried out on them.

We never had time!

This statement is particularly significant—usually made when the 'pressure is on'. One never has time to put it right when it happens, yet one always manages to find time for rectification later on when costs have escalated tenfold. This is surely not very efficient or cost-effective!

An effective and well-supported quality assurance programme would have gone a long way towards preventing the occurrence of the problem in the first place. 'Getting it right first time every time' is the maxim to adopt.

It has been quoted that the cost of maintenance work on an offshore platform amounts to approximately £10 million per annum. One could ask how much of this could be saved by 'getting it right first time'.

But we have always done it that way!

By thoroughly examining an activity it is almost always possible to find a much more efficient and cost-effective method of doing it. Probably most of us have never taken the trouble to find out whether a particular operation can be done more efficiently. Regardless of technological advances within a particular industry, the ability to assure quality has not kept pace. As has already been said, there is still a tendency to cling to these old methods of working, whereas companies should be looking at more efficient methods of achieving the desired quality. When reviewing current activities, a veritable Pandora's box of problems may be opened up.

Malpractices, inefficiency, duplication of activities, corner-cutting and high rework costs are just some of the short-comings that can be uncovered.

Personnel may see their jobs at stake and this can result in lack of co-operation, with the subsequent difficulties in implementing a quality assurance programme. Management must be firm and fair when committing itself to such a course.

When this list of statements and questions is examined, it should become apparent that the majority could have been procedurally controlled during the early stages of a project or contract.

COMMUNICATION AND CO-OPERATION

Communicating the problems, which have been experienced on previous projects or contracts, is of paramount importance, yet all too often it is not done. This may be due, in part, to the fact that at the end of a project or contract the team is disbanded and separated. No one person is aware of the totality of problem areas. The quality assurance manager is probably the ideal person to highlight these areas and to monitor the recording of such problems in corporate records. The corporate quality assurance programme should then be revised to eliminate recurrence on future contracts. This, of course, can never happen without top management and company dedication to quality assurance.

The customer can also play a very important part by debriefing the contractors at project completion. All too often problems are encountered, either during subsequent stages of a project or even after commissioning, which are not communicated back to the contractor, nor probably on to the subcontractors. This does not refer to major problems which are well advertised, but to those lesser problems which may result in unnecessary repair and maintenance costs, with possible production stoppages (which may well go towards the £10 million maintenance costs for offshore platforms referred to earlier).

This is an example of active customer–supplier relationship referred to at the beginning of Chapter 1.

It would be very difficult to quantify how many times one is greeted with: 'Quality assurance! What do we need that for? We have never had any problems. Our structure, facility, equipment, or whatever, has been operating for the past x number of years and is still operable.'

This may well be true but has anyone ever been advised what has been involved to keep it there and to keep it operating?

It is only recently, in what has become a very highly competitive world, that customers have begun looking more closely into quality costs. They now have the time and information to equate costs against previous project or contract performance and, in some cases, relate these costs with contractors' activities. The tender lists for new projects or contracts are a lot shorter than they used to be. If contractors fail to pre-qualify, they should look inwardly and start asking questions.

If it was necessary, in two words, to state the requirements of a successful quality assurance programme, the first would be 'communication'—which has already been stressed—and the second would be 'co-operation'.

It will become apparent in later chapters how much reliance is placed upon communication and how much dependence upon co-operation. The outcome can result only in cost-effectiveness, increased productivity, enhanced profitability and competitiveness, and go a long way towards 'getting it right first time, every time'.

4

Setting up and developing the appropriate quality assurance programme

THE RESPONSIBILITY FOR QUALITY

The senior executive of any organisation is responsible for two things: the efficiency of the company and the quality of the goods or services which that company offers.

In the larger organisation he will be ultimately responsible to the shareholders for the efficient running of the company and its profitability.

In the smaller organisation, where the senior executive may well be the owner of the company, he will have a responsibility to his employees, to his family and, in all probability, to his bank manager for the viability of the company.

FIRST CONSIDERATIONS

Any organisation, large or small, whether privately owned or not, can remain viable only if it continues to produce items or services which the customer wants and at a price the customer is prepared to pay. There are, therefore, two things which must first be considered when embarking on a quality assurance programme.

There is first the need to satisfy customer requirements by producing items or services which are fit for purpose, within budget and on schedule, and secondly the need to supply these items or services in the most efficient and cost-effective manner by introducing effective management systems, in addition to those of a quality assurance standard.

The need to satisfy customer requirements
This can be achieved by developing and implementing a quality assurance programme utilising the criteria given in the appropriate general quality

assurance standard, such as BS 5750, CSA Z299 or NS 5801/2. The requirement to implement a quality assurance programme to the industry-related quality assurance standards will, no doubt, have already been demanded by the purchasing body for that industry and will be a contractual obligation. There are, however, many instances where customers, other than those in safety-related industries, are demanding compliance with an appropriate quality assurance standard.

In any event, there are difficulties in meeting imposed requirements as most quality assurance standards are open to interpretation and misinterpretation. It is, therefore, recommended that, initially at least, any company embarking upon a quality assurance programme should use the available quality assurance standards as guidance documents only. Indeed, it may well be prudent to develop the quality assurance programme independently of the quality assurance standards, verify its implementation and effectiveness by audit and then determine with which quality assurance standard the programme complies.

The development of the appropriate programme will be dealt with in detail later.

The improvement in overall business efficiency

The criteria of the quality assurance standards are, in the main, directed at producing items and services which are fit for purpose. There are, however, many other functions over and above those specified in the quality assurance standards which contribute to the overall business efficiency of an organisation such as administration, secretarial, accounting, market research, maintenance, after-sales service and public relations. Shortcomings in any of these areas can lead to loss of business.

PUBLIC RELATIONS

In the widest sense, quality assurance should apply to the whole business activity—the total presentation—and not just to the product. In particular, this applies to what is nowadays called 'public relations' or PR. Just as most management systems are applied common sense, most PR is, in reality, just old-fashioned courtesy and 'good manners'. It is an area in which all too many 'quality-conscious' organisations fail. The items they produce can be of the highest quality yet, for example, if that organisation neglects to keep the customer informed of delays due to unforeseen circumstances, then that customer becomes agitated and with good reason. He expects to be informed of the reason for the delay; common courtesy demands it. Communication is of the utmost importance.

In the most common of situations when a bus or train is late, or fails to arrive, the traveller is most upset in being kept waiting without being told the reason for the delay or when transport is expected. A short communication by transport staff advising the reasons for a delay puts the traveller's mind at ease. Whilst he or she doesn't arrive at the destination any sooner, the psychological advantages of keeping the traveller informed are great.

The same thing applies to the late delivery of items or the late start-up of a service commitment. Keep the customer informed and it is realised that the company has the customer's interests at heart.

Management should also appreciate—but all too rarely does—that perhaps a company's most important members of staff are the receptionist and telephone operator—the links with the outside world. It is frustrating, and all too common, to be connected to an extension, via a switchboard, and to find that the extension remains unanswered and the caller left 'high and dry'. In such circumstances, the operator should be instructed to intercept the call and offer an alternative connection. This practice is carried out all too infrequently by many large and reputable organisations.

The reception area is another case in point. There are many instances on record where a visitor to a company is kept waiting, or worse ignored, while the receptionist finishes a private telephone conversation or is engaged in idle conversation with a colleague. Similarly, keeping a caller waiting is bad manners.

Such malpractices can have only an adverse effect on the overall business efficiency of an organisation and the elimination of them should, therefore, be included in any programme designed to increase the effectiveness, profitability and competitiveness of a company. A company must always be regarded as 'good to deal with'.

THE COST OF QUALITY

All companies employ someone to be responsible for the accuracy of its financial transactions and, in the main, that person occupies an executive post. That person is usually aware of the costs associated with such matters as absenteeism, holidays and down-time, and the senior executive will be obliged to present a complete financial statement to the authorities and, where necessary, to the company's shareholders. It is only rarely that a company will employ an executive who is responsible for quality yet, in many instances, a company's quality costs can be equal to, or even exceed, the profit margin of that company. Quality costs are generally not totally recognised.

A company will, in all probability, keep quite detailed records of goods returned under guarantee but will rarely be able to identify the costs of reworking substandard items, revising design drawings and specifications, repairing faulty structures due to poor welding, and others. Quality costs are the cost of putting things right! When an analysis is made of all associated costs, the result can be quite substantial. It should, therefore, be a requirement of every senior executive to realise what these costs are. The requirement to keep a detailed analysis of a company's financial affairs is required by legislation and yet, where the costs associated with putting things right are concerned, this is usually given scant attention.

In most manufacturing organisations there is a department which is given the responsibility for quality and, as has already been stated, this department is given a variety of titles all bearing the word 'quality'. In many instances, as we have seen, this department, although responsible for the control of the quality of the manufactured item, has no responsibility for verifying that all activities which preceded the manufacturing function were correct.

Companies should look towards the total integration and control of all activities; the *Gesamtkunstwerk* so to speak. This cannot be achieved by the department responsible solely for quality control or inspection, as the result will be only an increased activity in inspection and non-destructive testing, which, in turn, increases the costs of putting things right.

George Bernard Shaw wrote in his play *John Bull's Other Island:*

There are only two qualities in this world, efficiency and inefficiency;
and only two sorts of people, the efficient and the inefficient.

This statement has a great deal of truth in it. Efficiency is what every senior executive should be aiming for. The inefficient person is often inefficient because he or she is not happy with the work. That person is probably unsuited for the task being undertaken and management has not identified the problem. We are all fit for some purpose and we are all capable of undertaking some task or other efficiently. The problem lies in determining which task it is that the individual is best suited for.

Proper training can do much to increase efficiency, yet all too many companies do not recognise the fact.

Continuing with Bernard Shaw's definition, it could well be that quality assurance should be regarded as efficiency assurance. This being the case, then the responsibility for determining the efficiency of an organisation must be with someone much higher in the management structure.

It is, therefore, necessary when developing and implementing a quality assurance programme to appoint, in an executive position, a person who is to be responsible for the quality assurance function. The appointed person should have management capabilities and will be expected to be the guide, philosopher and friend mentioned earlier.

It is also essential for this person to be able to communicate at all levels. Knowledge and experience of the industry are essential requirements, as are the understanding and application of management systems. A knowledge of efficiency techniques would be an added advantage. This person, once appointed, would in effect represent the senior executive and would determine, with other management representatives, the functions to be controlled to achieve the required fitness for purpose.

ACHIEVING ACCEPTANCE OF THE QUALITY ASSURANCE PROGRAMME

As we have seen, an effective quality assurance programme involves all departments and functions. Such a programme can be developed only with the full participation and co-operation of all concerned, who must have the opportunity of helping to shape the programme. A programme that has been thoroughly discussed and agreed is much more likely to be accepted and implemented than one that is imposed—whoever does the imposing! It is worthwhile expending a great deal of effort in obtaining this co-operation and acceptance. It is necessary, therefore, for the respective department and/or discipline heads to be involved in determining the applicable programme level. This can be achieved, in the first instance, by forming a working party, which should comprise representatives from all the departments and/or disciplines concerned.

SETTING UP THE WORKING PARTY

The responsibility for the formation of the working party should lie with the person who has been appointed to the quality executive position. In order to place this person in the correct function, and to distinguish the position from that normally associated with 'quality'—that is quality control or inspection —it is perhaps worthwhile developing the Wagnerian concept of *Gesamtkunstwerk* still further by imagining this as the title for the department or the person concerned. In order to keep the title from becoming top heavy, one could then abbreviate it to GKW and our quality executive becomes the GKW director. By mentally transposing this title for quality assurance whenever it is used in this book it should become much clearer when differentiating between the person or department which controls the 'quality' of the hardware or service and the person or department which assures the quality of all the activities and functions which ultimately lead to the items and/or services being produced, not only fit for purpose but in the most efficient and cost-effective manner.

It is essential that the person who operates in the quality assurance (GKW) position represents the senior executive of the organisation and that he or she has independence of action.

All quality assurance standards, regardless of country of origin, place great emphasis on this point and, in general the criterion is that the person so appointed should preferably be independent of all other functions.

In the case of large organisations, this independence is comparatively easy to achieve and the quality assurance department will operate as a totally autonomous group but, with the smaller organisations, it is not possible to achieve this independence economically and it is in such instances that the *function,* rather than the *person,* should be defined. This will be dealt with in greater detail in Chapter 5.

The working party should be chaired by the senior executive of the organisation, with the quality assurance executive acting as the co-ordinator. This working party should include representatives from all the major departments and/or disciplines and these representatives should be, preferably, the heads of departments and/or disciplines. Where this is not possible, then the representative should be given power of attorney to act for the respective head.

ESTABLISHING THE APPROPRIATE QUALITY ASSURANCE PROGRAMME

The objective of the working party is to establish the appropriate quality assurance programme applicable to the organisation concerned. Before this can be done, experience has shown that it is usually necessary for certain actions to be taken, such as:

— To define responsibilities and lines of communication within each department or discipline.
— To establish inter-departmental interfaces.
— To verify and agree the activities and functions which are to be procedurally controlled.
— To communicate to all employees the reasons for, and the benefits to be obtained from, the implementation of a quality assurance programme.

Let us take each of these in turn.

Define responsibilities and lines of communication within each department or discipline

In many organisations a person's responsibilities are not clearly defined. There is a tendency to appoint someone to a given position and then to delegate additional responsibilities to that person as he or she becomes more proficient and experienced. As time goes on, this person reaches supervisory or management status purely by taking on these additional responsibilities and then, when things go wrong, it becomes exceedingly difficult to identify the cause or the source of the problem.

All responsibilities should be documented in the form of job descriptions, which should include as a minimum:

(1) The title or description of the position.
(2) The grade or level of the position.
(3) The reporting structure of the position.
(4) Whether or not the position carries any supervisory responsibilities.
(5) The primary responsibilities of that position.
(6) The knowledge and experience required to fill that position.

Fig. 4.1 gives an example of a typical format for a job description.

The activity of developing job descriptions will involve liaising with all employees and when the individuals are questioned on what they believe to be their responsibilities there will inevitably be duplications and overlaps. There could well be instances of activities not being completely covered as the demarcation lines had not been sufficiently clear and explicit. This in itself is, in the author's experience, the cause of many so-called quality problems.

The exposure and elimination of the duplication of activities is a sensitive area and must be done with care and consideration, otherwise it could well lead to ill feeling and resentment among employees who may feel that their

Typical job description

TITLE:	Here would be inserted the appropriate title for the position.
POSITION LEVEL:	Here insert the appropriate grading related to the position.
REPORTS TO:	Here would be inserted the person's immediate supervisor's position.
SUPERVISES:	Here would be inserted any supervisory responsibilities.
PRIMARY RESPONSIBILITIES:	Here would be inserted the primary responsibilities relating to the position, together with any interdepartmental interfaces.
KNOWLEDGE AND EXPERIENCE:	Here would be inserted the minimum qualifications and experience required adequately to undertake the requirements and responsibilities of the position.

Fig. 4.1 — Typical job description.

jobs are in jeopardy. This must not happen!

In addition to documenting job descriptions, it is advisable to formulate a promotion or career progression chart, which will tie in with the relevant grade or level of any given position. This information should be available to all employees and it will help in giving them a sense of belonging, which will inevitably lead to a greater responsibility to the company and ultimately achieving the efficiency required to produce the items and/or services fit for purpose and right first time, every time.

Once the job descriptions have been documented then, with the information which has been obtained, it will be possible to formulate organisation charts for each of the departments concerned. These charts will enable each grade, or level of employee, to understand and accept where their position is located within the hierarchy and to whom each person reports.

Establish interdepartmental interfaces
Organisation charts can be established for individual departments and/or disciplines but they will not achieve the integration of the total presentation-—*Gesamtkunstwerk*—if they are developed in isolation. No department can work in isolation. There is always the need to liaise with others. For example, sales must liaise with design, production and finance. An organisation chart which identifies these interfaces should, therefore, be developed. Where interfaces are established, then of course these would be documented in the appropriate job description and work procedure.

This detailed organisation chart will ultimately identify the primary positions and reporting routes of the company.

To verify and agree the activities and functions which are to be procedurally controlled
This activity will eventually determine the appropriate quality programme level and this is where the standards themselves give useful guidance.

The total activities or major activities of the organisation should first be listed. If a company is engaged in the design, manufacture and installation of a product, then each activity within each of these three elements should be itemised. For example, the control of design would cover such activities as:

(a) Establishing design parameters.
(b) Detailing the design.
(c) Design checking.
(d) Design approval.
(e) Control of design changes.
(f) Development of specifications.
      And others.

The control of manufacture would cover such activities as:

(a) Incoming inspection.
(b) In-process inspection.
(c) Non-destructive testing.
(d) Final inspection.
      And others.

DOCUMENTING THE QUALITY ASSURANCE PROGRAMME

When all the major activities have been identified, then a brief outline describing how these activities are controlled can be documented. These outlines assist in determining the procedural requirements, and they will also be utilised in the formation of the quality assurance manual.

A typical outline for some activities of design control is given in Fig. 4.2.

It will be noted from this outline that at least six subsidiary activities are involved in the control of design. These subsidiary activities should be controlled by means of individual procedures.

It will be seen that various 'levels' of documentation are being developed and, as pointed out earlier, these are:

System documents—which represent the overall function. The *act* in the total presentation.

Procedures—which detail how each activity within a system is carried out. The *scene*.

Therefore the outline for design control as a system outline can now be done. Similar outlines should be developed by each department concerned, including the quality assurance department itself.

The eventual responsibility of the quality assurance department will be:

(1) To verify the implementation and adequacy of the quality programme.
(2) To identify any deficiencies within the programme.
(3) To verify that corrective action has been taken to correct deficiencies and that action has also been taken to prevent a recurrence.
(4) To verify that personnel operating in the quality assurance function are adequately trained to carry out their activities.

A documented system outline would cover these points.

Fig. 4.3 sets out the system outlines that would be required to meet the criteria of the various quality programme levels.

It is to be understood that these are to be used as guidelines only, as there could be many activities related to a given programme level which a company need not implement. The two prime examples are purchaser-supplied materiel and sampling schemes. Most companies do not receive free issue materiel, neither do they require sampling schemes. Therefore, if they do not apply they need not be considered.

A control should not be implemented just because it is given in a quality assurance standard. These standards could be likened to the beef trolley in a restaurant. The customer selects only what he needs and leaves the rest! We are all aware that over-indulgence leads to obesity and an early death. Too many controls lead to bureaucracy and stagnation.

If a procedure doesn't do anything, if it is uneconomical to operate, if it gets in the way, if it produces unnecessary documentation, it is best forgotten!

Having documented the system outlines, the next step is to develop the procedure index.

As has been shown, each system outline will result in a number of activities which are to be procedurally controlled. These activities should now be listed and indexed.

All procedures should carry a document number as the procedures themselves will eventually form part of the company's document or library system.

Typical system outline for design control

1.0 The XYZ Company Engineering Department shall implement and operate design controls which shall provide for the following:

    1.1 INITIAL CHECKING OF DESIGN DOCUMENTS-—which shall define the responsibilities and general methods whereby design documents are subjected to a systematic initial check within the originating disciplines.

    1.2 INTERDISCIPLINE CHECKING—which shall define the responsibilities and general methods whereby documents with design interfaces are checked by the interfacing disciplines.

    1.3 AUTHORISATION AND REVISION STATUS/IDENTIFICATION OF DOCUMENTS—which shall define the necessary authorisation of documents including standard methods of adding and identifying revisions.

    1.4 INTERNAL DESIGN REVIEW—which shall define the responsibilities and general methods whereby documents are reviewed to identify progress.

    1.5 DESIGN INTERFACE CONTROL—which shall define the methods and responsibilities to control the interfaces between systems, contractors, regulatory authorities, etc.

    1.6 DESIGN FEEDBACK—which shall ensure that problems reported at all stages of a project, or contract, from manufacturing through assembly, installation, commissioning and servicing, receive attention in such a way as to avoid a repetition of past problems and promote future improvements.

2.0 Details of WHO, WHAT and HOW shall be defined in XYZ Company written procedures and work instructions.

NB: Design documents include drawings, specifications, data sheets, procedures, instructions, etc.

Fig. 4.2 — Typical system outline for design control.

Comparison between programme levels

	LEVEL 1	LEVEL 2	LEVEL 3
1. Quality programme	x	x	x
2. Organisation	x	x	x
3. Audits	x	x	
4. Quality programme documents			
—Manual	x	x	
—Inspection and test plans	x	x	x
5. Manufacturing control	x	x	
6. Planning (contract review)	x	x	x
7. Design control	x		
8. Documentation and change control	x	x	
9. Control of inspection, measuring and test equipment	x	x	x
10. Control of purchased materiel* and services	x	x	x
11. Incoming inspection	x	x	x
12. Purchaser-supplied materiel (free issue)	x	x	
13. In-process inspection	x	x	x
14. Final inspection	x	x	x
15. Sampling	x	x	x
16. Inspection status	x	x	x
17. Identification and traceability	x	x	
18. Handling and storage	x	x	x
19. Work instructions	x	x	x
20. Special processes	x	x	
21. Preservation, packaging and shipping	x	x	
22. Records	x	x	x
23. Non-conformances	x	x	x
24. Corrective action	x	x	
25. Training	x	x	x

*Materiel — collective noun covering equipment, stores, supplies and spares.

Fig. 4.3 — Comparison between programme levels.

A numbering system should, therefore, be developed which will identify the procedure to the department which implements it. Such procedures are not quality assurance documents.

A typical numbering system would be as follows:

XYZ-DE-001

where XYZ represents the company's initials, DE represents the design and engineering department, and 001 represents the document number.

The title of the document would also be identified, for example:

XYZ-DE-001 Design Validation

Procedures which are to be implemented by more than one department are normally of an administrative nature and could, therefore, be identified as:

XYZ-ADM-001 and so on

Once an index has been developed, it should be kept updated. If it is found that a particular procedure is no longer relevant and can be discontinued, then the number allocated to that procedure should be declared obsolete and not used again, the procedure index being annotated accordingly.

Once the system outlines and the procedures index have been developed, then it will be possible to relate the outlined programme to the relevant level.

The procedure index can also be utilised to identify those procedures which already exist and those which have to be written to complete the total presentation. The exercise of reviewing existing documentation may well highlight the existence of duplicate or similar documents, and possibly documents which are obsolete. This presents a good opportunity for reappraisal and a 'spring cleaning' session.

In essence, if an organisation carries out a design activity, then the eventual quality programme must be 'level one'.

If, however, no design function is carried out, or if manufacture is to an existing or proven design, then the quality programme will be 'level two', whereas if there is a requirement only for inspection and/or test, then the quality programme will be 'level three'.

APPLICATION TO SERVICE INDUSTRIES

The various quality assurance standards might at first glance appear to be solely applicable to manufactured items and that service companies would find them very difficult to apply, but this is certainly not the case.

If the 25 criteria of a typical 'level one' quality programme are analysed, it will be seen that many of them relate not only to manufacture but also to service industries.

For example (referring to Fig. 4.3), every company, regardless of the industry in which it operates, would require the following:

(1) Quality programme
(2) Organisation
(3) Audits
(4) Quality programme documents
(5) Planning
(6) Documentation and change control
(7) Control of purchased materiel and services
(8) Special processes
(9) Records
(10) Non-conformances

(11) Corrective action
(12) Training

Even the housewife, when making a cake, carries out activities which can be directly related to a quality programme standard. The various activities in cake-making are identified in Fig. 4.4

It will be seen from this simple process of cake-making that 14 out of a possible 24 'level two' activities are covered.

One could ask the question: 'What happens if the cook undertakes to make a cake to his or her own recipe?' This would then surely be a design activity and thus become a 'level one' programme.

This example is always popular at training courses. At one such course a delegate made the statement that corrective action had been taken but there was no evidence of any action taken to prevent a recurrence of baking an inedible cake. One can only conclude that such action would be to replace the cook!

IMPLEMENTING THE QUALITY ASSURANCE PROGRAMME

The final stage is the implementation of the programme. This will involve the co-operation of all concerned, and to obtain this co-operation all employees must understand the reasons for implementation.

Communicate to all employees the reasons for, and the benefits to be obtained from, the implementation of a quality assurance programme.
This is best done by holding a series of 'awareness' talks, or seminars, starting with senior management, through all levels to junior personnel. No one should be left out.

In the author's experience, co-operation is more easily obtained if these 'awareness' sessions are conducted before procedural controls are documented but after the quality manual has been written and approved. In this way all employees can prepare, and possibly highlight, problem areas which exist because of inadequate controls. By this means, personnel can be made to appreciate that they are part of the programme and that it will work to their benefit only if they co-operate.

The 'awareness' sessions, then, have the best impact if they are introduced after the quality manual has been written and approved. The manual should give supervisory staff, in particular, the broad outline of the programme within the area of their own involvement.

The requirement for review should also be emphasised and this review should include both system and compliance audits. The word 'audit' may frighten some staff as they may expect to be supervised continuously and suspect that management is adopting the 'Big Brother' attitude. It should be made clear to them that audits, as will be explained later, are carried out first to assess the adequacy of the system and only secondarily to verify compliance with instructions.

Quality assurance in making a cake (Level 2)

1.	Organisation	Who makes the cake
2.	Planning	Decide type of cake to suit the occasion (wedding, birthday, etc.)
3.	Work instructions	Recipe
4.	Records	Recipe library
5.	Control of purchased items	Ingredients—preferred brands, most economical source
6.	Manufacturing control	Mixing, blending, forming
7.	Control of measuring and test equipment	Scales, spoons, jugs, etc.
8.	Special process (heat treatment)	Baking
9.	In-process inspection (non-destructive testing)	Fork test, skewer test
10.	Protection and preservation of product quality	Storage/freezing
11.	Completed item inspection and test	Eating
12.	Control of non-conforming materiel	Consult the *Something went wrong—what do I do now?* cookbook* (material review board)
13.	Corrective action	Rework cake into a trifle
14.	Training	On the job training by parent or cookery lessons

*Bear, John and Marina (1970) New York: Harcourt Brace Jovanovich Inc.

Fig. 4.4 — Quality assurance in making a cake (level 2).

It should also be emphasised that each individual is responsible for the quality of the work produced and that reliance for quality cannot be placed on others subsequently to confirm that the required quality standard has been reached.

'Right first time, every time' should be everyone's goal. This is the prime goal of any quality programme, whatever its level.

COSTS AND BENEFITS

Developing and implementing a quality assurance programme will cost time and money. It is difficult to give estimates of costs, as these will depend on the size of the company and the complexity of its operations, whether or not any form of programme exists and on how many procedures are to be written and implemented. It would obviously be helpful if records of existing quality costs can be made available in order to enable an evaluation to be made of savings when the programme is in full operation.

Initially, there will be outlays related to: the time taken by the working party in establishing the requirements; the time taken in writing procedures; and the costs involved in the 'awareness' sessions. In a sense these costs can be regarded as capital expenditure and amortised against the substantial savings made in such areas as: revisions to engineering documents; rework on faulty items; scrap reductions; and others.

These costs have been plotted in a general format on the graph given in Fig. 4.5. It will be noted that, after the initial, in effect, capital expenditure, the cost declines rapidly and the costs associated with maintaining the programme should remain reasonably level. The savings made due to the implementation will rise initially and then remain effective so long as the programme is implemented.

A case history

To illustrate savings which can be made, and again drawing on the author's experience, an example relating to a design project may be used. Design is a service and there is no real tangible item on which its costs and benefits can be quantified in terms of reduced reworking, loss of production, or other factors.

In one particular project for a petrochemical pipeline design, the client imposed upon the design contractor the requirement to implement a 'level one' quality assurance plan. (As a project is being discussed, the quality assurance scheme is referred to as a plan.) The contractor was not conversant with the requirements and so it was necessary to develop and implement the required controls.

The contract was for a six-month duration, involving 15 design engineers. This presented a good opportunity to analyse quality costs, particularly as a similar project undertaken some time previously could be used as a cost basis for comparison.

During the previous project where 15 engineers were also involved, 650 design documents (drawings, specifications, data sheets) were produced and, on average, each document was revised three times. Each revision was found to take, on average, two hours. The total time spent on revisions,

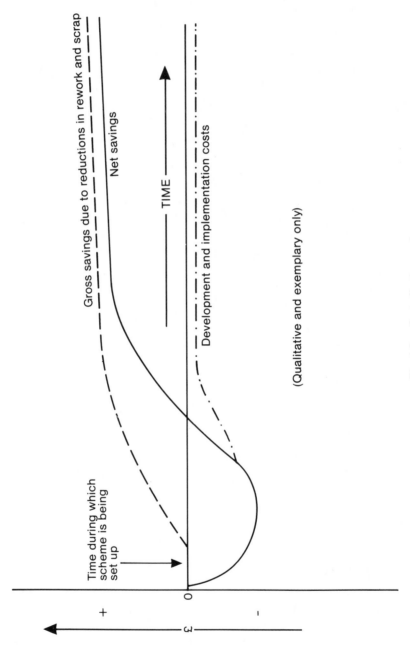

Fig. 4.5 — Cost-effective graph.

therefore, was $650 \times 3 \times 2 = 3900$ manhours.

During the later project where the 'level one' plan was implemented, it was found that the time spent on development and implementation of the plan was initially six weeks using three personnel, with intermittent subsequent involvement by one person to verify the implementation and adequacy of the plan.

The initial work-load was accordingly 720 man-hours. Verification of the implementation and adequacy of the plan took 2 man-days per week for 22 weeks, amounting to 352 man-hours, making a total of 1072 man-hours.

It was found that, at the end of the project, revisions had dropped by half, resulting in a saving of 1950 man-hours. To this should be added the reduction in time spent by the document reproduction department and the document control centre. The overall gross saving approached 2300 man-hours, giving a net saving of 1228 man-hours, when the costs are discounted.

When this was related to the total engineering budget of 14,400 man-hours, this represented a saving of approximately 9%, which may be considered a very good return for a first-time effort.

Implementation of the same plan in subsequent projects has reduced revision costs still further, thus placing this contractor in a much better competitive position than others who do not operate proper management systems.

It should also be taken into account that development costs for the quality assurance plan will be considerably reduced for future similar projects, provided that the lessons learned are properly assimilated and recorded in corporate records, so eliminating 'the reinvention of the wheel'.

5

The organisation for quality

THE IMPORTANCE OF ORGANISATIONAL FREEDOM

As will be seen from the quality programme comparison table in Fig. 2.2 all quality assurance standards place great importance on organisation.

BS 5750 makes the following comment:

> Practically all suppliers have quality control and/or inspection departments that are concerned solely with quality matters but these departments alone cannot satisfy all the requirements. Most other departments of a supplier's organisation are responsible for the achievement of quality. To establish a quality system that meets the requirement of BS 5750 Part 1 suppliers have to identify the functions and activities that directly affect quality and delegate to the personnel responsible for those functions specific authority to discharge that responsibility.

NS 5801 makes the following comment:

> The requirement that the contractor's manager for the quality department shall have organisational freedom, usually implies that he has an independent position in the organisation, with direct responsibility to the top management and is not charged with other quality influencing functions.

Canadian Standard Z299 makes the following comment:

> In the development of an organisation and the assignment of responsibilities and authorities it should be recognised that the quality program is interdisciplinary and involves most of the organisation. The responsibility for quality and assurance of quality cannot be considered the sole domain of any single group. Many functions and activities at all levels and divisions in the organisation are involved. Unless the responsibility for quality is fully acknowledged and understood by all from the top executive to the shop

worker full compliance with the Standard (Z299) cannot be achieved. Also, persons assigned responsibility for assurance of quality should be aware of but free from the pressure of cost and production and be given the necessary authority to perform their roles effectively.

All other standards make very much the same comment. However, what does it all mean?

QUALITY IS THE RESPONSIBILITY OF EVERYONE

It has already been determined that, ultimately, it is the senior executive of an organisation who must carry the responsibility for the quality of the items or services produced. The senior executive alone, however, cannot undertake every activity necessary to produce these items or services, unless of course it is a single-person organisation. There must be delegation of activities and in this delegation there must be the confidence that the employees are qualified, experienced and capable of carrying out the task for which they are employed. A certain amount of confidence is obtained at the initial interview but the confidence is sustained only if the employee continues to carry out his tasks in an efficient and effective manner. The senior executive cannot monitor all employees' performances on a continuous basis, therefore the confidence in the employees is maintained by the quality of the work produced.

The quality of work produced should not be determined by 'others'. There should be a fundamental requirement that everyone within an organisation is initially responsible for the quality of the work produced, and the assurance of quality should be practised by all personnel in their daily activities.

As this quality assurance—*Gesamtkunstwerk*—should be a company wide philosophy, then every department must organise itself so that the work produced is not only correct but, more importantly, correct first time.

This concept of *Gesamtkunstwerk* could be depicted as an umbrella which protects the organisation from the 'rain' of problems which could descend upon it. Fig. 5.1 shows such a concept. Beneath the umbrella are the various elements of a typical 'level one' organisation.

Each of these elements will require procedures to cover all the activities and functions within that element. Within each of these elements there should, however, be some means of verifying that the work carried out is, in fact, correct first time.

THE INDEPENDENT CHECK

Initially, of course, all employees should verify the quality of their own work by means of a self check. The accuracy of the work can then be confirmed as necessary by a controlling check carried out by a person suitably qualified but not directly involved with the activity.

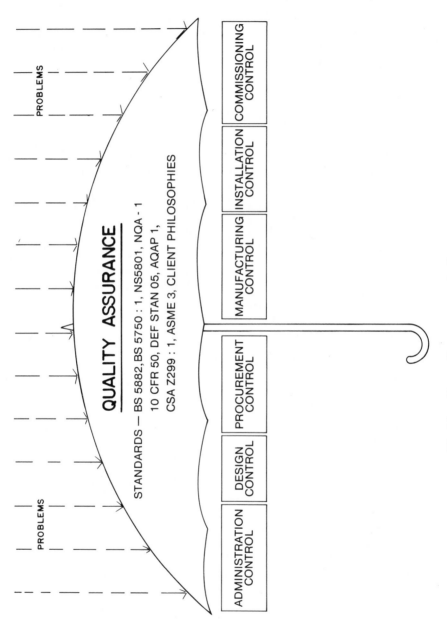

Fig. 5.1 — The quality assurance umbrella.

What has to be determined is who is to be responsible for controlling and checking the accuracy or quality of the work within each of the elements. In each case the responsibility for this can lie only with personnel who are familiar with that work if the check is to be effective but, in order to obtain an unbiased result, the check should be carried out by personnel not actually engaged in that activity. Checking is an activity in itself and should also be procedurally controlled.

If this checking function is to be effective so that no activity goes forward to the next activity in an incorrect manner and the check is to be carried out only by suitably qualified and experienced personnel, then:

— Design documentation can be properly checked for technical detail and accuracy only by design engineers.
— Procurement documentation can be properly checked only by personnel familiar with procurement activities.
— Manufactured items can be properly checked only by personnel familiar with the specification requirements.
— Installation activities can be properly checked only by installation engineers.

These requirements are, basically, only a follow-on from finance, where the accounting function of any organisation is checked, albeit a requirement by legislation, by qualified accountants.

Even those engaged in simple unskilled trades such as 'housekeeping' activities contribute indirectly to the eventual quality of an item or service and their activities should be similarly controlled and checked.

THE ROLE OF THE QUALITY ASSURANCE DEPARTMENT

Referring once again to Fig. 5.1, the quality assurance department would actually be located within the umbrella and would be responsible for:

(1) Verifying, by audit, that the *Gesamtkunstwerk* philosophy is being followed throughout the organisation and that effective procedures and work instructions are being implemented by all departments and/or disciplines.
(2) Verifying that those responsible for controlling and checking an activity have done so in a systematic manner and that there is objective evidence available to confirm such.
(3) Ensuring that all procedural non-conformances are resolved.
(4) Ensuring that fundamental working methods are established and that fully approved procedures are raised to cover them and that all departments and personnel are aware of, and have access to, current versions of these procedures.
(5) Verifying that all procedures are regularly reviewed and updated as necessary.
(6) Determining and reporting the principal causes of quality losses and non-conformances.

(7) Determining, with senior management, where improvements are required and, where necessary, recommending the corrective action.

By taking these actions a step further, it follows that the quality assurance department verifies that the organisation is implementing and adhering to the quality assurance scheme which, as has been determined, has been developed by management under the direction of the senior executive in conjunction with our quality assurance executive. The quality assurance executive and the department under him, therefore, act as the eyes and ears of the senior executive in determining that the company is operating in the prescribed manner and, should any problems arise, these can be dealt with effectively and efficiently.

Continuing with the umbrella analogy, the quality assurance department would, during verification activities, identify 'leaks' should these occur and would be instrumental in verifying that these 'leaks' are patched up by the appropriate department or discipline to prevent further 'leakage'. These 'leaks' could occur anywhere—over administration, over design, over manufacturing, and others. Hence the requirement of all quality assurance standards that the person responsible for quality should be preferably independent of other functions.

THE IDEAL ORGANISATION

The ideal organisation for a 'level one' company is shown in Fig. 5.2. This places the quality assurance function as a 'staff' function directly responsible to the managing director.

The quality control department is shown as reporting to engineering and design; the reasoning for this is explained later. In a 'level two' company, where there is no engineering or design activity, then quality control could well report to production.

This reporting structure, where quality control reports to production, may well be an anathema to some as it could be argued that, where there is a conflict between schedule and quality, then the quality control manager could well be overruled by the production manager.

In the author's experience, there have been instances where, in an organisation which had a reporting structure where quality control reported to the production manager but with no quality assurance department to keep a watchful eye on events, every Friday became a battle between the chief inspector and the production manager. The production manager would tour the manufacturing facility to determine which items were ready, but not released, for shipment. The fitness for purpose requirement was secondary; his philosophy being 'if it's wrong on delivery let the customer put it right and back-charge the rework costs to us'. Unfortunately, senior management also appeared unconcerned as they made no effort to support the chief inspector who wanted to delay shipment until the item was found to be

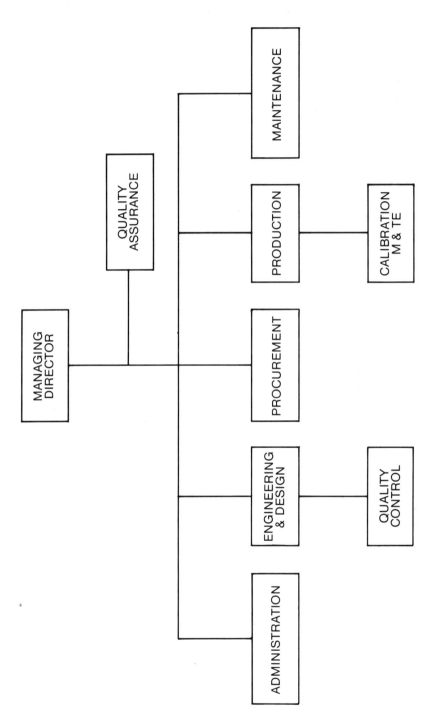

Fig. 5.2 — Ideal organisation for 'level 1' company.

correct. There was no commitment to quality by the works director; therefore there was no quality assurance representative to determine the implementation of, and adherence to, procedures. In fact, at that time there were very few recognisable procedures.

The prospect of receiving a large contract from the military, with a contractual requirement to implement a quality assurance scheme, soon made senior management see the error of their ways and, with a little assistance from the author, a suitable scheme was developed, which included reorganisation, so that responsibility for quality was placed on every department. The recommended reorganisation did, needless to say, upset many senior personnel, but the Friday battles instantly disappeared.

The organisation chart in Fig. 5.2 also shows the calibration of measuring and testing equipment as being the responsibility of the production department. This again may not be standard practice but surely it should be!

The production department should be responsible for the quality of its own work and should not rely on inspectors to determine subsequently whether the required quality has actually been obtained.

The production department will use measuring equipment to confirm sizes, tolerances and generally to control activities; then why should it not be responsible for the calibration of the equipment which it uses? The quality assurance department should be responsible for verifying that this calibration is carried out at the specified times and to the correct procedures. If discrepancies are found then the production department must take the necessary corrective action and prevent a recurrence. If subsequently there should be a recurrence of the discrepancy, then senior management would be required to resolve the matter.

Where a company places responsibility for the control of the measuring and testing equipment on the quality control or inspection department, the reason given, either implicitly or explicitly, is that the production department can not be trusted to do it properly. This lack of confidence in a vital part of the organisation certainly implies a failure to appreciate the whole ethos of quality assurance.

As was indicated in Chapter 4, the smaller company may not be able to support economically a separate quality assurance department. In such circumstances, the function of quality assurance could well be undertaken by others not directly involved with the activity.

TYPICAL (THOUGH NOT RECOMMENDED) ORGANISATION

Figure 5.3 identifies a typical company organisation where there is no identifiable quality assurance function.

In this type of organisation, the quality control department is responsible for the control of hardware and has, in all probability, been given an auditing function which many companies associate with quality assurance, hence the title QA/QC department.

In this organisational structure one must question who is to be respon-

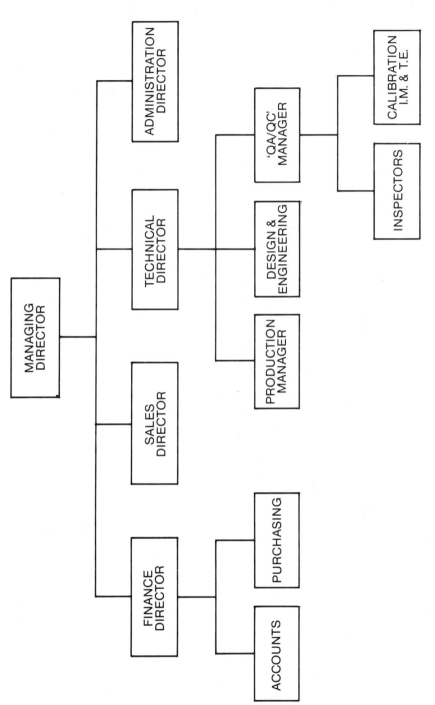

Fig. 5.3 — Typical (though not recommended) organisation of a 'level 1' company showing the possible location of the person responsible for quality.

sible for verifying that the QA/QC department is itself working to procedure. Also, in such an organisation, it is doubtful whether the other departments or disciplines—design, procurement, installation, and others —will accept this QA/QC department as the senior executive's representative. Experience has shown that, generally, this type of organisation has not been found to be effective, neither does it demonstrate a company's total commitment to quality.

How then can the smaller company deal with this situation?

The quality assurance function can still be identified as in Fig. 5.2 but the verifying activity can be undertaken by others in the organisation who are familiar with, but not directly responsible for, the activity under audit. This will mean, however, that the quality assurance function can co-opt others to act as the senior executive's eyes and ears, provided of course that such co-opted personnel are suitably trained and experienced. Alternatively, verification of compliance could be undertaken by a third party source.

Figure 5.4 shows a suitable organisation for a quality assurance department within a 'level 1' company.

As has been mentioned many times, it is the senior executive who is ultimately responsible for the quality of the items or services which the company produces, and for the efficiency and cost-effectiveness of the total organisation.

In a more direct manner, Fig. 5.5 shows how the umbrella concept operates.

QA/QC A MISNOMER

It has been established that, to be effective, the checking of an activity should be carried out by personnel who are familiar with, yet not directly responsible for, the activity.

Let us now analyse this further and, by so doing, determine that a quality control department cannot effectively be responsible for verifying the implementation and adherence of the quality assurance philosophy.

In essence, any type of checking activity could be equated with inspection. The accountant who checks the books is, in reality, inspecting them.

The design engineer who checks a design document is, in reality, inspecting it.

The buyer who checks procurement documents is, in reality, inspecting them.

Yet none of these 'inspectors' reports to the quality assurance manager. It is therefore illogical that, in the majority of organisations, the person who checks hardware, which is an inspection activity, should report to a manager of a department which is designated as QA/QC.

If the function of hardware inspection is analysed still further, it will be determined that the inspector carries out his check against a specification. Specifications are developed by engineers, therefore the inspector is acting for the engineer and should preferably report to him. Hence the organisation as shown in Fig. 5.2.

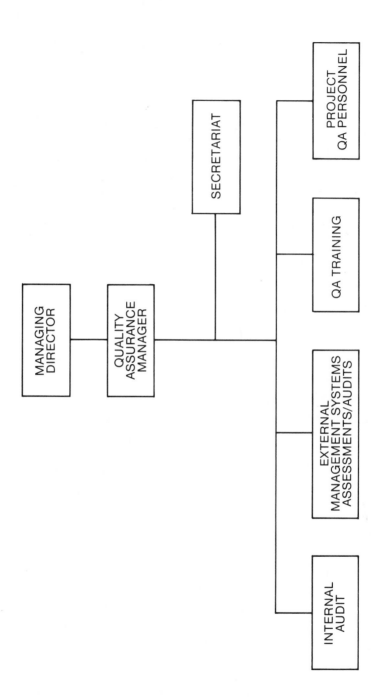

Fig. 5.4 — Quality assurance department organisation.

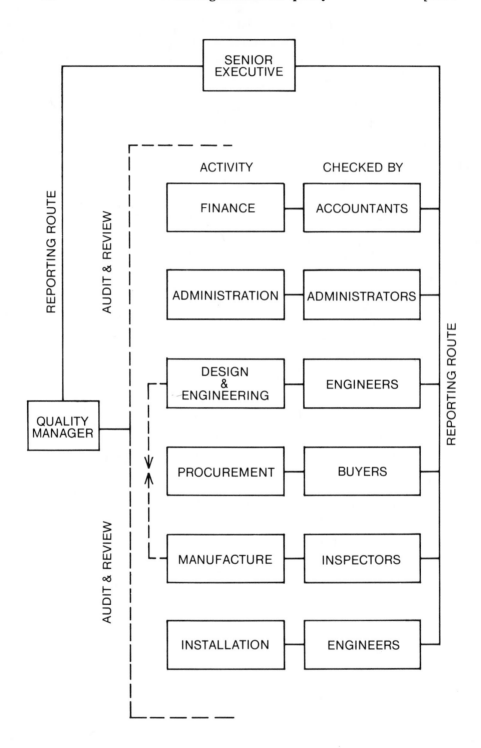

Fig. 5.5 — The checking functions.

Inspection or quality control could, therefore, be considered as the continuation of the engineering function, which is, as has been identified, just one activity within the total quality assurance — *Gesamtkunstwerk* — philosophy.

As with a change of government, the change of an organisation's senior executive could lead to a change of administration. This change could affect the attitude towards quality. If the quality assurance representative is of executive status, then this change in attitude will be minimised. If, however, the quality assurance representative is well down in the hierarchy, as in Fig. 5.3, the effects of such a management change could be disastrous.

The requirement for the quality representative to be preferably independent of other functions should now be well appreciated.

6

The policy statement

DECLARATION OF INTENT

Any declaration, such as a bill passed by Parliament, trade agreement, social contract, or similar pronouncement, becomes valid only when signed by a person, or persons, in the highest authority.

Similarly, any quality assurance scheme can be considered to have any 'teeth' only if signed by the highest authority in an organisation.

It will be, of course, necessary to formalise the intent of a quality assurance scheme into a document which is generally given a title such as quality manual.

The actual development and contents of a manual will be dealt with later, but there should be a signed declaration issued by the chief executive which signifies commitment to the documented quality assurance scheme.

As with any declaration of intent, it can be considered to be effective only in its actual implementation.

There are many instances, in all walks of life, where agreements or declarations of intent have been signed in all good faith but have been found not to be worth the paper they are written on, due to lack of implementation, caused by either the inability of the signatories to enforce the agreement or perhaps by a change in administration.

At least, in the quality-conscious company, the senior executive, in conjunction with his quality assurance executive, will have been instrumental in the development and implementation of the quality assurance scheme and should, therefore, be familiar with its contents. The senior executive should, if totally committed, therefore have no hesitation in signifying this commitment by appending his or her signature to such a declaration of intent. This declaration of intent is generally known as a policy statement.

The policy statement

The signed policy statement in a quality manual should give all employees and potential customers an initial indication of that company's intentions towards quality but, in order to determine the effectiveness of the quality assurance scheme, the customer could, and very often does, undertake an assessment or audit to verify that what is documented actually happens in practice. Similarly the senior executive maintains his confidence in the implementation and effectiveness of his own quality assurance scheme by means of internal audits, which are carried out by his quality assurance department.

A company's commitment to quality can, therefore, be judged initially by the strength of the signed policy statement and, subsequently, by management's attitude.

The policy statement, therefore, could be defined as:

A signed declaration issued by the chief executive of a company signifying that company's commitment to a given quality assurance scheme.

In the author's experience, a policy statement carries much more psychological weight if it is issued on the company's officially headed paper. In this format, it can then be used as a 'stand-alone' document in a variety of situations such as sales promotion, employee awareness, and others.

An example of a typical policy statement is shown as Fig. 6.1.

The general statement
In addition to the policy statement, it is useful to expand on quality responsibilities in the form of a general statement.

The general statement could, therefore, be defined:

An amplification of the policy statement issued to include quality responsibilities.

An example of a typical general statement is shown as Fig. 6.2.

There is no good reason why both statements should not be combined but, in the author's opinion, the combination of the two could detract from the impact of the policy statement as described earlier.

These two documents will be eventually included in the quality manual, the formulation of which will be dealt with in the next chapter.

The XYZ Engineering Company Limited
Alphabet House
Sigma Street
Beta Town
Fernshire

POLICY STATEMENT

The XYZ Company Limited specialises in the design, procurement, manufacture and installation of specialised equipment, supplying mainly to high technology markets. The nature of the company's activities places particular emphasis upon experience, expertise, capability, reliability and quality.

The prime objective of the management of The XYZ Company Limited is to provide this equipment and the associated services in a manner which conforms to contractual and regulatory requirements.

In order to achieve this objective, it is the policy of The XYZ Company Limited to establish and maintain an efficient and effective quality assurrance programme, planned and developed in conjunction with all management functions. Determination of conformance of work to contract and regulatory requirements is verified on the basis of objective evidence of quality.

The quality assurance programme of The XYZ Company Limited is based upon the requirements of... [here would be identified the applicable quality assurance standard: BS 5750, part 1; NS 5801; CSA Z299.1 and others].

The XYZ Company Limited's quality manual, and the systems outlined therein, describe how the quality assurance programme of The XYZ Company Limited is designed to ensure that all quality and regulatory requirements are recognised and that a consistent and uniform control of these requirements is adequately maintained. The XYZ Company Limited's quality manual also defines how effective control is established.

A. PERSON
Managing Director

Fig. 6.1 — Policy statement.

GENERAL STATEMENT

The assurance of quality is fundamental for all work undertaken by The XYZ Company Limited and is practised by all personnel in their daily activities.

Quality is enhanced by working in a systematic manner to formalised procedures designed to eliminate the occurrence of deficiencies.

To promote a uniformity of work method throughout, irrespective of client requirements, certain procedures fundamental to The XYZ Company Limited shall be implemented at all times, without significant deviation.

It shall be the responsibility of the individual Department and Discipline Managers to compile, implement and integrate the requirements of these procedures into their regular working methods, and to ensure that all such methods are clearly defined and documented.

It'shall be the responsibility of The XYZ Company Limited's management to ensure that these procedures are implemented and consistently and regularly reviewed to reflect current customer and Company philosophies.

It shall be the responsibility of the Quality Assurance Department to monitor constantly the implementation of the current quality assurance programme in order to verify that the necessary systems, procedures, etc., exist or, in the absence of such, to determine that they are raised and to verify implementation and adherence by regular auditing.

The Quality Assurance Department shall be so organised as to be free of commercial/contractual restraints and to represent The XYZ Company Limited on all matters relating to quality assurance.

Fig. 6.2 — General statement.

7

The quality manual

The quality manual was touched upon briefly in Chapter 2, where it was described as a document setting out the general quality policies, procedures and practices of an organisation.

WHY A QUALITY MANUAL IS NEEDED

In addition to the fact that most quality standards indicate the requirement for such a document, there are a number of other very good reasons for its production.

It is a very good management 'tool' to keep employees aware of their responsibilities within the quality programme; it can thus become a suitable training document.

Its use can reduce the 'learning curve' due to employee turnover and can thus assist in the continuity of events in such cases.

It can, if well written, become a useful addition to the 'sales aids' of an organisation, as it will outline a company's intentions with regard to satisfying the customer by producing items and/or services which are fit for purpose.

The use of a manual as an effective training document has been proved on many occasions during the author's experience.

In Canada there are many major purchasers who require proof of the effective implementation of a quality assurance scheme by a supplier before the supplier is included in the bidders' list. The quality assurance scheme is related to the appropriate level of CSA Z299.

A case history may be of some interest. There was one particular supplier who was at a loss to fulfil the requirement of Z299.3 (Quality Verification Program Requirements) but was anxious to be included on the bidders' list for a major contract soon to be let. The author was engaged as a consultant to this supplier. One of the major problems encountered by this supplier was in the requirement for inspection. It was his understanding of the Standard that he would be required to engage an additional person as an inspector as the Canadian Standard Z299.3 clearly stipulates:

> The use of competent persons for inspection other than those performing or directly supervising the work being inspected.

With a staff of only twelve personnel this apparent demand for extra staff would increase production costs and seriously affect competitiveness. However, it was pointed out that, to meet the requirements of the Standard, it was not necessary to engage any more staff as in no instance does the document state that the supplier shall have a separate or independent inspection group. It is quite satisfactory for the inspection to be carried out by another member of the work-force, provided he, or she, has the knowledge and ability to do so, and provided the person performing the inspection was not directly involved in the work.

This was just one area of misinterpretation of the requirements. There were a number of others which will not be discussed here.

The supplier eventually developed and implemented a 'level 3 quality verification program' which met the requirements of the Standard and which was assessed and approved by the buyer, with the end result that this supplier not only attained the bidders' list but was also awarded a contract.

A few months later, on a follow-up visit, it was found that a different shop foreman had been appointed. The supplier advised that this had not really affected productivity as the quality manual, together with the relevant procedures, enabled the new foreman to assume his position with the minimum of training and indoctrination. The 'learning curve' had been considerably reduced and, in just this one instance, the initial cost of developing and implementing the quality programme had been more than recouped.

THE SHOP WINDOW TO QUALITY

The quality manual could be described as a company's shop window to quality. It is to the company as the display window is to a store. The items in the store window will indicate to a prospective customer the nature and quality of the merchandise which the store has for sale and, in order to appreciate the totality of its stock, the customer will venture inside and purchase whatever it is that is required.

Similarly, the quality manual describes a company's intentions towards satisfying the fitness for purpose criteria and the prospective cutomer, as for the merchandising store, can venture inside the company and verify that company's commitment to quality by auditing the programme.

The quality manual, therefore, states in general terms the methods used by a company to assure quality. It is, as has already been indicated, a document of intent, describing 'what' is done to assure quality. The detailed procedures, which should be available at the activity locations, will describe, in addition, the 'who', 'how', 'when', 'where' and, possibly, 'why' of an activity.

MANUAL FORMAT AND CONTENTS

There is no defined format for a manual. The presentation of the document is a matter of personal choice but, in essence, it should be designed so that it is easily updated.

As described in Chapter 4, all activities and functions which require to be controlled should be collated into system or procedure outlines. These outlines describe in general terms what is required to control a given activity and it is these outlines which form the basis of a quality manual.

As a guide it is recommended that a manual comprises three sections, as follows:

(1) Company quality policy
   — policy statement.
   — general statement on quality objectives.
   — statement on quality assurance authority and responsibility.
   — details of company and quality assurance organisation.
   — statement on the manual amendments, reissue and distribution.
(2) System outlines
   — outlines of systems addressing the applicable criteria of the company's quality programme.
(3) Procedures index
   — an index of the company's procedures.

Let us take each in turn.

Section 1   Company quality policy
This section should be devoted entirely to describing the company's commitment to quality and would include the following:

(a) The policy statement, which has been described in detail in Chapter 6.
(b) The general statement on quality objectives, which also has been described in detail in Chapter 6.
(c) A statement on the authority and responsibility for quality assurance. This would detail the organisation for quality as related to the requirements of the company but, wherever possible, it is to be emphasised that the person appointed should have the necessary authority and responsibility to ensure that the company's quality programme is being implemented and adhered to by all concerned. Such responsibility will normally mean that the person so appointed should be of management status and should be preferably independent of other functions. The quality assurance authority statement will describe this, and a typical statement covering such authority would read as follows:

Authority and responsibilities
Department and Discipline Managers
With regard to quality, all Department and Discipline Managers shall be responsible for:

(1) The quality of work carried out by all personnel within their respective departments or disciplines.

(2) Verifying that approved procedures are adopted within their department or discipline and that any necessary complementary procedures are established, implemented, reviewed and updated ·as required.

(3) Ensuring that all staff are adequately qualified and experienced in their relevant discipline to perform the duties of their position in a satisfactory manner.

(4) Ensuring that all staff are familiar with company procedures and have ready access to them.

Quality Assurance Executive

(1) The Quality Assurance Executive is the final authority and represents the Company on all quality matters pertinent to the quality assurance programme as established by customer requirements, regulatory requirements and company quality policies and procedures. The Quality Assurance Executive reports directly to the Managing Director.

(2) The Quality Assurance Executive has the primary responsibility to structure the quality assurance programme, which will involve all company departments and/or disciplines in a focused effort to ensure compliance with quality requirements.

(3) Specifically the Quality Assurance Executive is involved in areas such as:

— Drafting company policy on quality.
— Setting company quality objectives.
— Reviewing the organisational relationships as they affect quality and developing proposals for improvement.
— Determining and reporting the principal causes of quality losses and non-conformances.
— Monitoring the company's quality assurance programme to determine where improvements are needed and recommending, as necessary, the appropriate corrective action.

(d) The details of company and quality assurance organisation normally comprise organisation charts which show:

— The company organisation with departmental/discipline reporting lines. This chart should be developed to show the relationships, interfaces and hierarchical structure of the various departments or disciplines.
— The quality assurance organisation with its independence from other functions.

Typical charts for both company and quality assurance organisations are as Figs. 5.2 and 5.4.

(e) The statement on amendments, reissue and distribution should

indicate how amendments to the manual are dealt with. It should also
indicate what is done to control the distribution of the manual.

Controlled and uncontrolled conditions

Manuals, as for most other documents, are issued under *controlled* and
uncontrolled conditions.

Controlled conditions imply that the document is given a serial number
and allocated to a specified person. The recipient of the manual acknow-
ledges receipt and is provided automatically with amendments and reissues.

Uncontrolled conditions imply that the document is issued for information purposes only and so will not be kept updated. It is in a company's
interest to keep 'controlled' documents to a minimum. One should establish
'need to know' rather than a 'want to know' distribution list. A typical
statement on amendments, reissue and distribution could read as follows:

Amendments, reissue and distribution

The XYZ Company Limited's Quality Assurance Department reviews
this manual periodically with other departments and disciplines to re-
affirm its adequacy and conformance to current requirements of the XYZ
Company Limited. The maximum period for review of the manual is once
yearly.

Amendments to the manual are made as required to reflect the
current quality assurance programme. The amendments are made by
replacement of the applicable page(s). Each amended page is identified
by amendment number and date of amendment.

Amendments are numbered consecutively until such time as a new
issue incorporates all such changes. When changes affect a considerable
number of pages, and in any case after not more than ten amendments to
one issue, the manual is reissued. Issues are identified by numbers in
numerical order. Each issue cancels and replaces all previous issues and
amendments.

The amendment list indicates all the amendments to the latest issue of
the manual.

A complete list of quality assurance manual holders, together with the
amendment records, is retained by the . . . (here would be inserted the
department responsible for the function, i.e. Quality Assurance Department, Document Control Department, Library, or others). Amendments and reissues of the manual are automatically distributed to all
registered holders.

It shall be the responsibility of all registered manual holders to update
the manual assigned to them and to destroy obsolete copies of all
amended pages.

Section 2   System outlines

This section should contain brief outlines of the primary functions of the
company's quality assurance programme as determined by both company
and customer requirements.

It should include the controls to be exercised on those aspects of the function which have an effect on quality to ensure conformance to customer requirements. The systems outlined should not only reflect current quality policies but should also take into consideration the requirements of national and international standards and regulations related to quality assurance programmes, such as BS 5882; BS 5750.1; ANSI/ASME NQA-1; NS 5801 and CSA Z299.1.

Unless the company is very small with few functional controls, the inclusion of detailed procedures within a manual is to be avoided. There are three very good reasons for this:

(1) Procedures are 'living' documents and are continually under review. Experience has shown that a procedure cannot be considered to have attained its full 'maturity' with regard to content, acceptability and effectiveness until it has reached revision four. If procedures are included in the manual updating becomes a very costly and laborious process. If, however, procedures are kept separate from the manual, then any procedural amendments would be an independent exercise which would have no effect on the outlines in the manual.

(2) The majority of the recipients of a manual would not generally be concerned with the detailed aspects of a given activity or the technicalities of its operation. Detailed procedures would, therefore, be just additional pieces of paper for which they will have no use.

(3) Procedures are proprietary documents which have taken a great deal of time and effort to produce. They are for company use only and should not be made freely available to third parties. Procedures should generally be made available only to those who are to implement them.

There is, of course, the inevitable exception to the rule. When procedures are developed to meet certain customer requirements, the customer will invariably wish to review them to determine their compliance with certain contract conditions.

To illustrate points 1 and 2, the author during one particular consultancy was requested to review the company's quality manual, which at that time was a bulky document of 140 pages. The manual contained, among other things, a very detailed procedure covering the auditing of the quality programme. As this was the most detailed document in the manual, it was evident who was responsible for quality in that organisation—certainly not the senior executive as he appeared to leave all such matters to his quality manager.

The manual was issued under 'controlled' conditions to 44 individuals and that particular procedure was at revision 3. The procedure itself comprised nine pages; therefore a great deal of unnecessary paper (in fact almost 1200 pages) had been distributed to personnel who had no direct responsibility for auditing. Most of the recipients of the manual were not involved in the auditing function and would not therefore need to know the techniques but only to know that auditing was in fact carried out.

An outline of the auditing function is all that should have been required in the manual, the detailed procedure being made available to those who had a responsibility for auditing. It was later established that, apart from the quality manager, all others who had some responsibility for auditing were neither recipients of a 'controlled' copy of the manual nor did they have an up-to-date copy of the procedure.

What however is even more enlightening was the number of manuals issued under 'controlled' conditions. Of the 44 copies, ten were distributed to customers, the remaining 34 being issued to members of staff. The total work-force of that company was only 130, which meant that 26% of the work-force were on the 'controlled' distribution list. One can only assume from this that the 'want to know' rather than the 'need to known' philosophy prevailed. The responsibility for updating the manual, in this case, must have approached a full-time occupation. Generally it should be necessary to issue manuals under 'controlled' conditions only to management and per- haps supervisory staff. They, in turn, should be made responsible for keeping their staff informed of the manual contents.

The outcome of this consultancy resulted in the redevelopment of the manual, which became a much slimmer document of just 37 pages, with the 'controlled' distribution reduced to seven. The procedures were made available at point of use.

The system outlines should follow a logical sequence and should cover all aspects of the relevant criteria of the company's quality programme.

Whereas the outlines should logically follow the same sequence as the quality standard with which it is intended to comply, this can present a problem when supplying items or services on an international basis, as the majority of standards do not apply a uniform index. The need for a formal presentation of documents is a *sine qua non* of any quality assurance scheme, yet nations do not practise what they preach when it comes to interchangeability of quality standards.

In any event, once an organisation has established and implemented its own quality programme, and continually verifies its effectiveness, there is no reason why it should not meet all international standard requirements for the applicable level. There may be additional requirements 'imposed' by a customer to meet certain safety and/or environmental regulations but these requirements can be adequately taken care of when developing a quality plan for that project or contract.

A typical systems outline index would be as follows:

Contract review (planning)
Design control
Change control
Traceability control
Document control
Control of purchased materiel and services
Purchaser supplied (free issue) materiel
Control of special processes
Identification of items

Non-conforming items
Corrective action
Inspection, test and operating status
Control of inspection, measuring and test equipment
Handling and storing items
Preservation, packaging and shipping
Incoming inspection
In-process inspection
Final inspection
Records
Audits
Training

The contents of various system outlines will be established in the applicable chapters which relate to the various elements for control.

Section 3   Procedures index
This section should include the procedures for all the systems and functions applicable to a company's own quality assurance programme.

While it is generally necessary to include only those procedures relevant to a given quality programme level, it is worthwhile indexing procedures relating to all management functions. Such an index will then assist the work-force in determining the correct procedure for any given function.

The information listed in this section should include the document title with the relevant document number. The author does not recommend the inclusion of procedure revision status as this can lead only to unnecessary updating of this section.

Procedure revisions should be controlled by the responsible department. Procedures, as for any document, should carry an identification number to facilitate control. A typical numbering sequence for procedures would be the tripartite system as follows:

XYZ-MAN-001

In this example, the company's identity is represented by the first three letters (in this case the XYZ Company Limited). The department or function is represented by the second set of three (in this case MAN refers to Management) and finally the three digits refer to the procedure number.

The following is a typical, but by no means exhaustive, procedures index:

MANAGEMENT AND ADMINISTRATION
Sales and marketing	XYZ-MAN-001
Public relations	XYZ-MAN-002
Review of quality system	XYZ-MAN-003
Communications	XYZ-MAN-004
Safety policy	XYZ-MAN-005
Contract control	XYZ-MAN-006
Minutes of meetings	XYZ-MAN-007

Personnel training	XYZ-MAN-008
and others	

ENGINEERING

Design criteria control	XYZ-ENG-001
Design document validation control	XYZ-ENG-002
Engineering change control	XYZ-ENG-003
Traceability control	XYZ-ENG-004
Interface control	XYZ-ENG-005
Weight control	XYZ-ENG-006
Design review	XYZ-ENG-007
Requisitions	XYZ-ENG-008
Specification preparation	XYZ-ENG-009
Computer-aided design	XYZ-ENG-010
and others	

DOCUMENT CONTROL

Document numbering and identification	XYZ-DOC-001
Procedures preparation—style and format	XYZ-DOC-002
Development, approval and implementation of activity documents	XYZ-DOC-003
Procedures index	XYZ-DOC-004
Document storage and retrieval	XYZ-DOC-005
Operating manuals and dossiers	XYZ-DOC-006
Records/certification	XYZ-DOC-007
Document revision and distribution	XYZ-DOC-008
and others	

PLANNING

Contract review meetings	XYZ-PLA-001
Progress reporting	XYZ-PLA-002
Work activity packages	XYZ-PLA-003
and others	

PROCUREMENT

Vendor assessment	XYZ-PRO-001
Tender package development	XYZ-PRO-002
Bid package review and evaluation	XYZ-PRO-003
Supplier selection	XYZ-PRO-004
Purchase orders	XYZ-PRO-005
Expediting	XYZ-PRO-006
and others	

QUALITY ASSURANCE

Quality manual	XYZ-QA-001
Audits—internal/external	XYZ-QA-002
Audits—extrinsic	XYZ-QA-003
Corrective action request	XYZ-QA-004
Auditor qualification and training	XYZ-QA-005

MANUFACTURING
    Material control   XYZ-MNF-001
    Special processes   XYZ-MNF-002
    Identification of items   XYZ-MNF-003
    Non-conforming items   XYZ-MNF-004
    Handling and storage   XYZ-MNF-005
    Preservation, packaging and shipping   XYZ-MNF-006
    Control of inspection, measuring
        and test equipment   XYZ-MNF-007
    and others

QUALITY CONTROL
    Incoming inspection   XYZ-QC-001
    Purchaser-supplied materiel   XYZ-QC-002
    Inspection, test and operating status   XYZ-QC-003
    In-process inspection   XYZ-QC-004
    Final inspection   XYZ-QC-005
    Hold activity notification   XYZ-QC-006
    Non-destructive testing   XYZ-QC-007
    and others

INSTALLATION
    Mechanical installation   XYZ-INS-001
    Electrical installation   XYZ-INS-002
    Instrument installation   XYZ-INS-003
    Pipework fabrication and erection   XYZ-INS-004
    Protective coating   XYZ-INS-005
    Cathodic protection   XYZ-INS-006
    Pressure testing   XYZ-INS-007
    Special processes   XYZ-INS-008
    and others

As can be seen from the above, when procedures are related to the function they are intended to control, very few are actually the responsibility of the quality assurance department. In many organisations, all procedures are regarded as quality assurance procedures, which can only confirm the lack of understanding of quality assurance concepts.

In summary, one should endeavour to keep the manual simple. It is, as has already been emphasised, a document of intent.

The inclusion of any information which is likely to be subject to continual amendment should be avoided. Procedures are one example of details not to be included; organisation charts are another. It is recommended that titles or functions, and not the individuals names, be indicated on such charts. Titles or functions, once established, do not normally change but individuals most certainly do!

In the introduction to this book it was stated that 'quality assurance is not a massive paper generator'. It will not be if one exercises adequate controls on information and adopts the 'need to know' rather than the 'want to know' doctrine. By employing the efficiency techniques referred to earlier, the majority of individuals presently engaged in what is loosely termed 'quality engineering' could make their jobs easier and probably much more satisfying and rewarding.

8

The procedure

Now that the system outlines have been developed and incorporated into the quality manual, the next step is to produce the detailed procedures.

Procedures, as have been said, comprise the real evidence of quality and should be considered mandatory for any quality assurance scheme.

In order to document any activity, one must understand how that activity is carried out and how each step within a given activity leads into the next step. When documenting any activity the actual act of writing it down can highlight anomalies, duplications, lack of important interfaces, and so on.

The understanding of how each activity is carried out must point to the fact that procedures can be considered only as representing a true account of an activity if they are written by the personnel actually carrying out that activity.

It also goes without saying that once an activity is 'proceduralised' it facilitates review by others who may have an involvement in that activity and any changes in the activity will be automatically documented. Documented changes will highlight to all concerned at the same time that such a change has been made. Documented changes will also act as an audit trail in the event of information being required at a later date to verify when and why an activity was amended.

Procedures will also assist in reducing the 'learning curve' when employee changes are made.

FORMAT

As has already been said, all procedures to be effective should be consistent in their presentation and should carry the same contents list.

The author favours a six-section presentation which comprises 'purpose', 'scope', 'references', 'definitions', 'procedure' and 'documentation', and it is this six-section format which is to be used as a guide.

It is strongly recommended that, when documenting an activity, the future imperative 'shall' rather than 'will' is used in the third person. This stresses the importance of the activity and that it is to be carried out without exception. 'Shall' is mandatory, 'will' signifies an intention and, as is well known: 'The road to hell is paved with good intentions'.

CONTENTS

Utilising the agreed format, which in this case would be the six-section format indicated above, the contents would be as follows:

Purpose
This section outlines the objective or intention of the document. For example, if a procedure is being written for document control then this section could read as follows:

> The purpose of this procedure is to provide instruction and to assign responsibility for controlling by a systematic sequence of actions the issue, receipt and withdrawal of all documents and revisions thereto associated with the accomplishment of any work activity and the achievement of quality objectives, specified either by contract or company objectives.

Scope
This section will outline the area, department, group or personnel to which the procedure applies. Again, using the document control procedure as our model, the scope would read:

> This procedure is applicable to all documentation generated as a result of implementing the requirements of either the quality assurance programme of the XYZ Company Limited or a quality plan developed by the XYZ Company Limited for a contract.

References
Here would be detailed other documents which have a bearing on the acitivities within the procedure. For example:

Document number	Title
XYZ-QA-001	Quality assurance manual
XYZ-DOC-001	Document numbering and identification
XYZ-DOC-002	Procedures—preparation, style and format
XYZ-DOC-003	Development, approval and implementation of activity documents
XYZ-DOC-004	Procedures index

Definitions
This section defines a word or action not readily understood. Again, using the document control procedures, here are some examples of definitions:

Documents

Shall include procedures, specifications, drawings, work instructions, correspondence either individually or collectively.

Procedure

A document detailing the purpose and scope of an activity and specifying by whom and how it is to be properly carried out.

All other definitions are as BS 4778 'Glossary of terms used in Quality Assurance'.

Procedure

This section would detail the actions of those personnel involved in the activity. It should also state wherever possible, who does what and how, where, when and possibly why the activity is carried out.

The effectiveness of a procedure can be determined by taking each clause of this section to see if it will turn easily into a question. This is an aid to auditing. For example, using the document control procedure once again, there may be a clause which reads:

All documents retained in the master file shall be filed in lockable fire-resistant filing cabinets.

This can easily be changed to a question by prefixing the statement with 'Are' and omitting 'shall be'. If this clause is being implemented then, of course, the answer would be 'yes'.

Documentation

This section lists any documentation referred to within the procedure and generated as a result of implementing the procedure. A copy or example of each such document should be attached to the procedure as an appendix. It facilitates control if any documents which relate to a given procedure carry a reference number which links that document to the procedure.

To qualify this, it is assumed that the document storage and retrieval carries the number XYZ-DOC-005, then any supporting forms would be numbered DOC-0051, DOC-0052 and so on. In this way it makes for extreme simplicity when identifying which procedure governs a particular document, and vice versa.

General

It is important that the procedure index always follows the same format without variation. In the event that, for example, there are no references, then under the section entitled References in the procedure the word NONE should be inserted. There is nothing worse than producing similar documents each with the index in a different order.

For reference, an example of a typical procedure for writing procedures 'Procedures—Preparation, Style and Format' is appended to this chapter.

Document Number
XYZ–DOC–002

Document Title

PROCEDURES—PREPARATION, STYLE AND FORMAT

Revision 1

Page 1 of 5

Fig. 8.1

INDEX

1.0 PURPOSE
2.0 SCOPE
3.0 REFERENCES
4.0 DEFINITIONS
5.0 PROCEDURE
6.0 DOCUMENTATION

XYZ-DOC-002
                                                               Rev 1

Fig. 8.2

1.0 PURPOSE

1.1 The purpose of this procedure is to describe the method of preparation, style and format of all procedures established for use by the XYZ Company Limited departments and/or disciplines.

This procedure shall be used as an example of such preparation, style and format.

2.0 SCOPE

2.1 This procedure shall apply to all documents which identify the activities and functions of a department or group and shall be observed by all XYZ Company Limited departments and disciplines without exception.

3.0 REFERENCES

3.1 XYZ–DOC–001 Numbering system for XYZ Company Limited documents.

3.2 XYZ–DOC–003 Procedure for development, approval and implementation of activity documents.

3.3 XYZ–DOC–004 Procedures index.

4.0 DEFINITIONS

4.1 Procedure

A document that details the purpose and scope of an activity and specifies how it is to be properly carried out.

5.0 PROCEDURE

5.1 Authorisation to proceed

The need for a procedure shall be identified by the department or discipline Manager concerned and the development of such agreed with the appropriate discipline Head (refer document XYZ–DOC–003).

Fig. 8.3

5.1.1 Once the requirement has been agreed and an author delegated, the author shall obtain a definitive procedure number from the document control centre (refer document XYZ–DOC–001). This procedure number shall be unique for the procedure to which it is to be applied and shall not be used to identify any other document. In the event that the decision to proceed with the procedure is rescinded, then the document control centre shall be so advised and the number reinstated for future use.

5.2 Procedure format

5.2.1 The cover page of the procedure shall be in accordance with form DOC–0021 (see attachment number 6.1) and completed with the following information:

— Document number
— Document title
— Cover page/revision status
— Revision and approval box

Refer to the cover page of this procedure for standard format.

The cover page shall always be identified as page 1 of—.

5.2.2 The procedure's index shall always appear as page 2 of—.

5.2.3 The index page and all subsequent pages of the procedure shall be completed using XYZ standard bordered stationery (see attachment number 6.2). Each page shall be identified by number and shall carry the appropriate document identification and revision in the bottom right-hand corner.

5.3 Procedure content

All procedures shall carry the same content which shall be as follows:

5.3.1 Purpose—which outlines the object or intention of the document.

Page 4 of 5   XYZ–DOC–002
                                                           Rev 1

Fig. 8.4

5.3.2 Scope–which outlines the sphere, department, group, or personnel to which the procedure is applicable.

5.3.3 References—which detail other documents which have a bearing on the activities within the procedure.

5.3.4 Definitions—which explain a word or action not universally understood, or which may have a specific interpretation in the procedure.

5.3.5 Procedure—which details the actions of those personnel involved in the activity. This section shall identify wherever possible who does what and also how, when, where and why the activity is carried out.

5.3.6 Documentation—which lists any appendices referred to within the procedure.

5.4 The procedure's index shall always include the content as detailed in clause 5.3 above (see attachment number 6.3). There shall be no variation. In the event that, for example, there are no references or definitions, then under the applicable heading the word NONE shall be inserted.

5.4.1 In the event that additional details are required to be incorporated as a supplement to the procedure, then these shall be incorporated as an appendix to the procedure.

6.0 DOCUMENTATION

6.1 Procedure cover page.

6.2 XYZ Company Limited standard border stationery.

6.3 Procedure index page.

Page 5 of 5

XYZ–DOC–002
Rev 1

Fig. 8.5

Document Number

_____

Document Title

_____

Cover Page/Revision Status

Page 1 of   XYZ–DOC–002
Form No. DOC–0021   Attachment No. 6.1

Fig. 8.6

Form No. DOC–0022   XYZ–DOC–002
Attachment No. 6.2

Fig. 8.7

INDEX

1.0 PURPOSE
2.0 SCOPE
3.0 REFERENCES
4.0 DEFINITIONS
5.0 PROCEDURE
6.0 DOCUMENTATION

Page 2 of   XYZ-DOC-002
Form No. DOC–0023   Attachment No. 6.3.

Fig. 8.8

9

The quality plan

As was seen in Chapter 2, the quality plan is the quality assurance scheme developed for a contract or project. It is developed from a company's quality programme and should include any unique requirements applicable to a given contract or project.

The quality progamme, which will by now have been developed, comprises the quality manual together with the detailed procedures covering all the activities and functions of an organisation. Imagine these on a shelf in a bookcase (Fig. 9.1). The quality manual should be a document comprising,

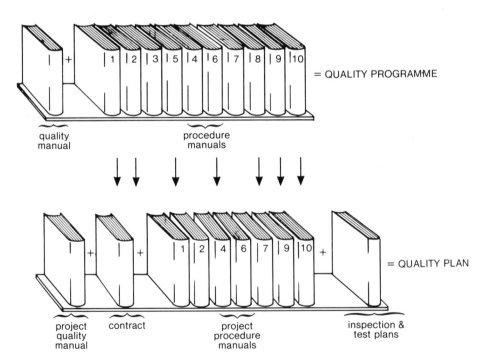

Fig. 9.1 — Bookshelf.

at most, forty pages. The procedures themselves, perhaps fifty, sixty, or more of them depending upon the size of the company and the complexity of its operations, should comprise an average of ten pages each. It is usual to keep all procedures relating to a given subject together under one cover. For example, all those relating to design would be kept together; similarly those relating to procurement, manufacture, quality control, administration, and so on, ending up with a series of what could be termed procedure manuals. The procedures index as described in Chapter 7 gives a good indication of the number of procedure manuals that may be required.

The quality manual, plus these procedure manuals, would then make up a company's quality programme.

A complete quality programme should be kept by very few people within a company. Generally, the only people who would need to be on a distribution list for the complete programme would be those who are concerned with all aspects of the programme. In the main, these would be: the senior executive himself, as he and his management team would have been instrumental in the development and implementation of the quality programme and would need to be aware of all activities and functions; the quality assurance manager, as he and/or his department would be responsible for verifying the implementation and adequacy of the quality programme; and the person or department responsible for distribution and control of such documents. Again the 'need to know' rather than the 'want to know' philosophy should prevail.

THE REQUIREMENTS FOR A QUALITY PLAN

This then is the quality programme but a company can remain in business only if it has work to do. The work it does may be of a general and continuous nature and, once the quality programme has been developed, it could remain continuously viable, apart from routine revisions, perhaps to update working practices or to increase efficiency.

In other circumstances, however, particularly in project-related industries such as civil engineering, power production or petrochemical, a company may be required by contract to undertake certain activities outside the normal scope of its work activities. Conversely, it may be required to undertake only some of the activities within its total scope.

For example, in the first case there could be a contractual requirement for a company to implement identification and traceability of materiel which normally it does not do. This would have to be covered by the development and implementation of a system to cover such an activity for this contract only.

In the second case, a company could be involved in the design, manufacture and installation of certain items of equipment and would have a quality programme designed to meet the requirements of a 'level one' quality programme standard but could win a contract for the manufacture of equipment designed by others. It would be necessary in this case to extract from the quality programme only those procedures relating to the manufacturing activities and incorporate into them any contract requirements for additional testing, inspection and the like.

FUNDAMENTAL PROCEDURES

In all circumstances there will be activities which will be common throughout all contracts. They are fundamental to the operation of the company and cannot, and should not, be turned off and on at will. This, unfortunately, is not always the case. There have been a number of instances in the author's experience when undertaking an audit where the auditee has very proudly shown him a production line which operates a 'level two' quality programme. On questioning the auditee regarding other production lines, the answer has been: 'Commercial quality only—the customer doesn't call up any quality standard'. What a philosophy! Once a quality programme is installed, it should operate automatically and become so ingrained into everyone's activities that it is a fundamental process. If a customer fails to call for a quality system, this should not be an excuse not to implement one. The type of activities which are fundamental, regardless of customer requirement, comprise such functions as:

Administration
Finance
Document control
Record storage, retention and retrieval
Planning (contract review)
Corrective action
Audits
Training
Customer liaison

This list is not exhaustive.

It surely must be totally uneconomic to switch the control of these activities on and off. What does it cost not to implement a system, notwithstanding the confusion which such a philosophy must cause?

Having said that, then, in the second case, the manufacturing controls applicable to the contract would be automatically supported by those fundamental procedures such as described above. The quality plan would, therefore, address all applicable elements and those procedures unique to the contract would be so identified and amended as necessary to suit. A case in point is the identification of documents. Many customers require a contractor to utilise a contract or project-related numbering system. This must be taken care of within the applicable procedure.

Another instance could be a requirement for a specific test on a piece of equipment. This would need to be documented but, as it relates to hardware rather than to a system, it would be documented in an inspection and test plan, which will be described later.

CONTRACT REQUIREMENTS

In order to develop the quality plan, it is apparent that one must be very familiar with the requirements of the contract work scope; therefore initially a contract review meeting is most important. All activities and functions relating to the contract should be planned. This applies to any type or level of activity—planning is of the utmost importance yet it is surprising the number of quality standards which address this activity only in relation to a 'level one' quality programme. It should be a fundamental activity regardless of quality programme level. The scope of such a planning activity is dealt with in later chapters.

Once the contract has been reviewed, then it can be determined which procedures are necessary to control that contract and which of those already established procedures will need to be amended or modified to suit certain contract requirements.

Where required by contract, a contract quality manual should be established in the same manner and format as the corporate quality manual but, in this instance, the policy statement would be signed by the contract or project manager.

CONTRACT ORGANISATION

The contract or project organisation may well differ from that shown in the corporate quality manual and should therefore be identified. Figures. 9.2 and 9.3 are typical charts showing a total project organisation and the quality assurance function within a project. It should be noted that the quality assurance representative within a project, although initially reporting to the project or contract manager, also has a functional reporting route outside the project back to the corporate quality representative through to the senior executive. Notwithstanding the fact that the project or contract manager has signed the policy statement, the ultimate responsibility for quality still lies with the senior executive and the project manager must himself comply with, and implement, the quality practices of the company.

To emphasise the importance of the contract review meeting as a means of familiarising the contract or project team with the contents of the contract, a case study is well worth considering.

There was an occasion when the author was employed as a quality assurance manager by a major contractor. This contractor had received a telex from a customer advising that a major design contract was about to be placed with him. The formal signing of the contract was to take place on a predetermined date. It was made known to this contractor that a quality plan was to be developed and implemented within six weeks of contract start date. Initially a project quality manual was to be produced and submitted to the customer for review and concurrence within 14 days of contract start-up.

Although only a telex of intent had been received, the project manager designate felt it would be worthwhile preparing the project quality manual beforehand and so save time once the contract was signed.

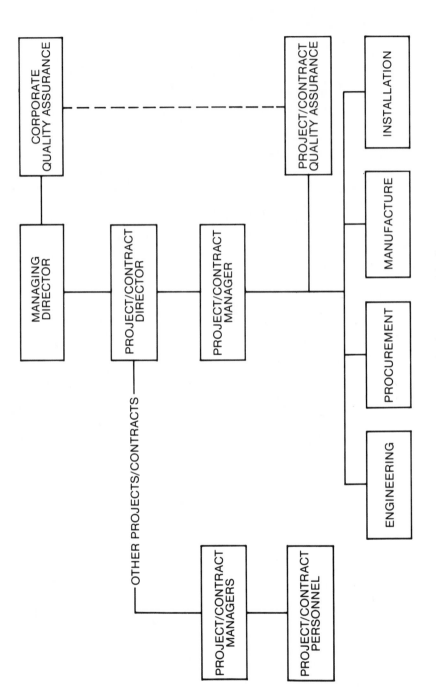

Fig. 9.2 — Project/contract organisation.

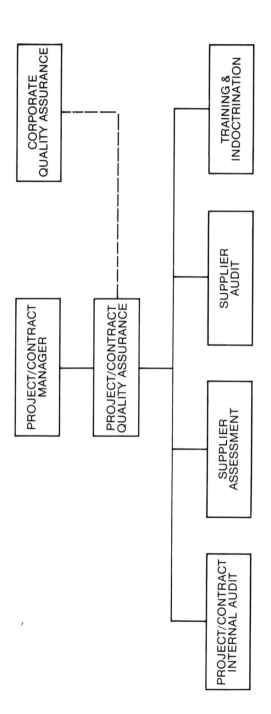

Fig. 9.3 — Project/contract quality assurance organisation.

The quality assurance manager was requested to establish such a document so that it could be handed to the customer on the same day that the contract was signed. He accordingly requested the project manager designate for information on the work scope of the contract. This was not available! The quality assurance manager, therefore, said that he was unable to write a project quality manual until the full work scope was known but, because of limited responsibility within the contractor's organisation, the quality assurance manager was virtually ordered by senior management to comply with the request.

Reluctantly the quality assurance manager set about the task of producing the manual on the work scope given orally to him—this being design, procurement and inspection. This meant developing system outlines for such activities as:

Document control
Design control
Change control
Traceability
Reliability
Maintainability
Control of purchased items and services
Internal and external audits
Quality control
Corrective action
Training

The manual was duly completed and handed over to the customer well in advance of the required date.

The project manager was happy because he had beaten the first schedule milestone. The quality assurance manager was very unhappy because he had produced a document under duress, with which he was not satisfied and he had made this known to senior management who had seen fit to ignore the protest.

The worst, however, was yet to come. The contract commenced without the contract team together reviewing the work scope; each lead engineer went about his business in complete isolation, convinced that each knew exactly what his own discipline's involvement was.

The customer, having received the manual, arranged to audit the system as outlined in the manual.

Half the work-force was found not to be in possession of the detailed procedures indexed in the manual. The actual work scope was design only and did not include procurement and quality control activities. In fact, when an analysis was made with regard to percentage compliance, it was found that this contractor was only 40% in compliance with the quality plan as presented in outline form in the manual. The production of the quality manual was a contract requirement and legally the customer could have held that contractor to its contents—particularly as it had received the project manager's approval. The customer, fortunately, chose not to take such a course of action and requested the contractor to revise the manual in line with the contract work scope.

In fact, the customer confirmed that the manual did not reflect the true work scope and should not have been written until the work scope had been established by contract.

If the contractor's senior management had listened to its own quality assurance manager in the first place, then the contractor would not have been placed in such a predicament. There is a good deal of evidence in support of the view that it frequently takes an outside third party source to add credence to a decision or statement made by an employee. The very first documented evidence of such goes back almost two thousand years. The Apostle John wrote: 'For Jesus himself declared that a prophet is without honour in his own country' (John 4: 44, New English Bible).

In this particular case, the quality assurance manager's standing within that organisation immediately increased and from then on he reported direct to senior management and henceforth could no longer be overruled by a project manager in matters of quality assurance principles and practices. No longer did this contractor pay only lip service to quality requirements as had been the case before this event.

Two lessons emerge from this case study: first, the need to conduct a contract review meeting; secondly, a confirmation of the need for the independence and authority of the person responsible for quality.

THE PROJECT QUALITY MANUAL

The contents of the project quality manual should, therefore, reflect details of the contract work scope and generally follow the same format as for the corporate quality manual. There will be some differences, as follows:

(a) The policy statement will reflect the quality policy of the project and will be signed by the project or contract manager.
(b) Responsibilities will be defined to reflect the requirements of the project or contract.
(c) The organisation will relate to the project and may include customer representation.
(d) The amendments and reissue will conform to contract requirements.
(e) The system outlines will address the applicable criteria of the quality standard specified in the contract.
(f) The procedure index will identify only those procedures applicable to the contract.

AS for the corporate quality programme, once the system outlines have been developed, the supporting procedures can be identified and then taken from the corporate programme and used as they stand or amended to suit contract requirements and, where necessary, new procedures written to cover activities not normally undertaken.

The manual, plus the supporting procedures, then become the contract or project quality plan.

10

The inspection and test plan

The quality plan, as described in Chapter 9, could be summed up as a series of documents which serve to direct the activities of personnel assigned to a contract or project.

As has been seen, corporate procedures which are used on contracts or projects may require modification to suit certain contractual requirements, although almost certainly many procedures will require no modification as they are fundamental to everyday activities.

Similarly, in a manufacturing environment there are standard methods of controlling production activities and these activities are formalised in a document known *generally* as an inspection and test plan. The word generally is italicised as the document described in this chapter may unfortunately be given many other titles, such as—'quality control plan', 'quality assurance plan', 'quality plan'—thus adding to the confusion in terminology and to the misunderstanding of quality assurance which presently obtains.

In instances where production of an item is standardised and unvarying, the inspection and test plan should be a standard document indicating the inspection and test requirements relating to the item. In many instances, however, the customer may specify additional inspection and test requirements over and above those stated in the standard documents so as to satisfy certain safety or regulatory requirements or, perhaps, to satisfy some special requirements of the design engineer.

EVIDENCE OF SPECIFIED REQUIREMENTS

At all times it will be necessary to specify in-process and final inspection and/ or test requirements. These requirements should be planned in order to provide objective evidence that the manufacturer of an item is proceeding, or has been completed, in accordance with the specified requirements. In all cases, so as to reduce subsequent rectification work, the responsibility for the 'correctness' of a manufacturing activity must lie with the person who does the work. This person should not rely on the activities of others subsequently to verify such 'correctness'. The 'self-check' is the first link in the 'assurance chain'.

In all too many instances in the manufacturing environment, 'inspectors' physically remove an item from a machine (lathe, milling, planing, or the like), take it to an inspection bench to check dimensions and surface finish—reject it and return it to the operator who realigns the item on the machine and rectifies the fault. The inspection process is then repeated to verify corrective action. This is a waste of time and effort! Surely it would have been more effective and productive for the operator to have first checked his own work; then, if an independent inspection was required, to have the inspection carried out 'in situ'. This approach is by no means uncommon. It also occurs in areas other than manufacturing.

In project management the author has often been presented with a pile of engineering documents and has been asked: 'Have these been quality assured?' The question is best left unanswered.

It should now become apparent that the inspection and test plan bears a certain relationship to the quality plan, as does the quality control activity to the quality programme.

The quality programme and the quality plan are both total presentations related to the company and the contract or project quality assurance scheme respectively. The quality control activity and the inspection and test plan are both related to 'hardware'.

THE NEED FOR AN INSPECTION AND TEST PLAN

The inspection and test plan describes, therefore, the inspections and tests specified for a given item.

The contractor may well be manufacturing many different items for a given contract, or market-place, in which case inspection and test plans for each of the items could be required. These plans will form only part of the quality plan (the total presentation), as many activities over and above actual manufacturing should be controlled, such as design (where necessary), procurement of materiel and services, document control, records, auditing, training, and so on.

It is not unusual for a customer to request the submission of an inspection and test plan for his approval or concurrence before commencement of manufacture. Such submission gives the customer the necessary confidence, or otherwise, that due consideration has been given by the contractor to any special inspection and/or test requirements specified by him.

There are also many instances where the customer may well formulate his own inspection and test plan for a contracted item and impose the requirements upon the contractor. In either event, it should be clearly indicated in the tender documents what is required. It should not be left until the contract has been placed, as this leaves the way open for the contractor to start claiming 'extras'.

FORMAT AND CONTENTS

The inspection and test plan, as with any series of documents, should be of uniform presentation. As with quality manuals and procedures there is no defined format. The presentation is again a matter of personal choice, but it should contain certain basic information, which, as a minimum, should include:

(1) Inspection and test points.
(2) Inspection requirements.
(3) Mandatory hold points (customer and regulatory).
(4) Sampling schemes (where required).
(5) Applicable standards.

Let us take each in turn:

Inspection and test points

Each inspection and test point should be determined together with its relative location in the production, shipping, installation and commissioning cycle. In the case of small consumer items, there may not be an installation and commissioning activity, but where there is, then there should be a facility for inspection and/or testing during such activities.

Unfortunately, inspection and testing during the installation and commissioning activity is something very often neglected by so called 'quality conscious' companies—particularly those in the building industry. Double glazing, home extensions, central heating, are some which spring readily to mind.

Once the item has been manufactured, the installation and commissioning work is often subcontracted and the prime contractor absolves himself of any further responsibility. If the contract is to supply (manufacture), deliver, install and commission then, regardless of any activities which may be subcontracted to third parties, the prime contractor is responsible all the way down the line and should 'build in' to his own inspection and test plan the necessary controls to assure confidence that each activity in the production, delivery, installation and commissioning cycle is not only right but also right first time, every time.

Inspection requirements

At each specified inspection and/or test point the requirements of such inspection and/or test should be detailed, either in whole or by reference to a particular inspection and/or test procedure. Details of any special equipment required for the inspection and/or test should also be indicated, together with any related qualification/experience criteria of inspection personnel.

Acceptance and rejection criteria should be indicated.

Details of any customer inspection points should also be indicated and a system established for liaison with the customer when such inspection points are scheduled.

Mandatory hold points

In many safety-related industries there are mandatory requirements that certain items or processes must be verified, by an approved third party source, as meeting minimum legal requirements. In order that the certifying or regulatory body can determine that such requirements have been met, in certain instances it is necessary to inspect and/or test at predetermined critical 'milestones' during production or installation.

In such instances there will be a requirement imposed on the contractor by the customer that once these defined 'milestones' have been reached no further work should be carried out until the certifying or regulatory body has verified acceptability and has issued a formal instruction to proceed.

Such 'milestones' are given the title *Mandatory hold points*. These hold points should be suitably documented or 'flagged' in the inspection and test plan in an 'eye-catching' form. To fail to notify the certifying or regulatory body that such a 'milestone' has been reached could result in, at worst, the item being refused its certificate or, at best, undoing all the work carried out after the mandatory hold points—reverting to bare metal, so to speak.

These hold points should be established in agreement with the certifying body and all responsible personnel made aware of the problems which could arise when failing to notify the appropriate regulatory authority. It is essential, in such instances, that the appropriate interfacing personnel should be identified in project records.

Sampling schemes

Where used, or where specifically required by contract, sampling schemes should be indicated and the location in the manufacturing cycle where they are used should be specified. Reference to published sampling plans should also be indicated. Where applicable, batch or lot sizes should be defined. The acceptance and rejection criteria related to sampling schemes should be also laid down.

Applicable standards

All applicable related standards and procedures should be indicated within the inspection and test plan, together with the latest applicable revision status.

The inspection and test plan is an official document and should be identified and controlled. Amendments to such plans should be procedurally controlled, with the responsibilities for updating and revising being clearly defined.

In some situations it could be a contract requirement that, in the event of amendments, these should be submitted to the customer for approval or concurrence.

Fig. 10.1 is an example of an inspection and test plan document.

INSPECTION & TEST PLAN

Page   of

CUSTOMER:	CONTRACT NO.	EQUIPMENT DESCRIPTION:		IDENTIFICATION/ROUTE CARD NO.					REGULATORY BODY

A table titled "INSPECTION & TEST PLAN" with columns:

INSPECTION POINT NO. | INSPECTION/TEST DESCRIPTION | INSPECTION/TEST CHARACTERISTICS TO BE VERIFIED | APPLICABLE DOCUMENT-ATION | ACCEPTANCE CRITERIA | QUALITY CONTROL (H W R) | CUSTOMER (H W R) | REGULATORY BODY (H W R) | AUTHORISATION (1 — QC; 2 — CUSTOMER; 3 — REG. BODY) with rows 1, 2, 3 repeated

Legend and Instructions:-
H=Mandatory hold point. Customer/Regulatory Body to be advised 7 days prior to the inspection and test point being reached. No further operations to be carried out until Customer's authorisation to proceed is received.
W=Witness point. Quality Control and Customer/Regulatory Body to be advised.
R=Review of documents required.

| REVISION | |
| APPROVAL | |

XYZ-QC-008.1

PLAN NO.

Fig. 10.1 — Inspection and test plan.

The contents of a quality programme and a quality plan have now been defined. It is hoped by now the reader will have a firm understanding of what the total presentation of a quality assurance scheme covers. It is now time to look at the various elements or acts within this total presentation. The first 'act' to be dealt with is design control.

11

Design control

It is regrettable that most expertise in what is termed quality engineering currently lies in controlling the quality of manufacture, and a great deal of time and effort is spent in assessing manufacturers' abilities to control their own quality. Manufacturers can be assessed and audited regularly and, indeed, they often are. In fact, it is not unknown for a single manufacturer to be audited or assessed a dozen times in as many months.

But what do such activities tell the customer? Only how good this manufacturer's systems and controls are. Yet, if the design is in error, this manufacturer, even though his systems and controls are more than adequate, will present the customer with hardware which is unsuitable for the service requirements.

At the risk of stating the obvious, it is therefore essential for the design to be right before placing the specification with a manufacturer. This means that not only should the design be correct but it should be correct first time. In order for this to be achieved it is necessary to put design controls on a formal basis and to develop a quality plan which meets the needs of the contract scope of work. It is worthwhile considering how an engineering department or design contractor can use quality assurance as a means of controlling design.

The first problem facing an engineering department or a design contractor is that, in the main, industry has not as yet agreed the need for, let alone a uniform approach to, quality assurance. Existing quality programme standards are not completely comprehensive as far as engineering design is concerned. While such standards as BS 5882 and ANSI/ASME NQA.1 go a long way towards meeting design control requirements, they would be generally unacceptable to most of industry because of their nuclear connotations. Therefore some of the controls discussed here will not be found in all of the quality programme standards, yet they do reflect what is perhaps becoming the general custom and practice.

DESIGN PROCEDURES AND INSTRUCTIONS

The procedures, methods and instructions to be utilised on a project or contract will probably comprise corporate documents, amended where necessary to suit specific contract requirements. In all cases, these contract procedures should be reviewed and approved by the appropriate contract manager in conjunction with the quality assurance manager and the relevant discipline or department manager. The customer will very probably wish to see and review them also and give his agreement before they are released.

Each manager of an engineering department or design contractor should be responsible for maintaining up-to-date procedure manuals for his area of management, including procedures for:

(1) The checking of such documents as drawings, data sheets, calculations and specifications.
(2) The control of design or construction work by the use of philosophies, procedures and standards.
(3) Standard preparation methods for specification, data sheets, drawings and work packages.

Each lead discipline engineer or supervisor should ensure that all significant activities are properly conducted and documented throughout a contract or project, verifying that:

(a) All necessary data, specifications, standards and other documents are available before the start of any activity.
(b) All the required work, drawings, reports and calculations are in fact produced during each activity.
(c) All the required checks, reviews and audits are carried out on completion of each activity.
(d) Any deviation from the above requirements is properly documented.
(e) All documents are systematically numbered or otherwise identified, filed, updated as required, and held securely in a system which ensures that they are readily available upon request to assist reviews or audits by the contract or project team, the relevant corporate discipline manager, quality assurance staff or the customer's representative.

THE MAJOR ACTIVITIES

The controls considered to be the most important in a design activity have been compiled for ease of reference into a tabulated form (Fig. 11.1).

It will be seen that this table is divided vertically under four headings, as follows:

Design control activity—which is self-explanatory.
Scope—which identifies the scope of work within that activity.
Performed by—which identifies those involved in, and who are responsible for, that activity.
Action by quality assurance—which summarises the responsibilities of the quality assurance department to verify that the activity is being, or has been, effectively implemented and controlled.

DESIGN CONTROL			
DESIGN CONTROL ACTIVITY	SCOPE	PERFORMED BY	ACTION BY QA
1 Contract review	Review: Work scope Specifications and standards Philosophies Design criteria Regulatory requirements Organisation	Project management Discipline engineers Quality assurance	Verify that missing or ambiguous information has been followed up and satisfactorily closed out by the responsible person
2 Document preparation, control and retention	Ensure correct and uniform presentation of documents. Ensure formal preparation, identification, checking, approval and distribution, including amendments. Verify retention, retrieval, storage and hand over requirements	Project management Discipline engineers (Customer)	Audit adherence to procedure
3 Discipline check	Verify content and accuracy of documents originating from own discipline	Relevant discipline	Audit adherence to procedure
4 Interdiscipline check	Assure compatibility of design between design disciplines. Accuracy of content	Project management Discipline engineers	Audit distribution and approval. Verify as necessary that comments have been closed out by the originating engineer
5 Internal design review	Review of design activities in progress or completed	Project management Discipline engineers Quality assurance	Verify that comments have been closed out
6 Design interface control (see also 4)	Check physical interfaces between systems/contractors, authorities	Project management Discipline engineers (Other contractors) (Customer)	Audit distribution and approval. Verify that comments have been closed out
7 Change control	Check changes in design criteria	Project management Discipline engineers	Monitor, changes as required, to close out and approval
8 External design reviews	Detailed audit of design — Adequacy of design — Adherence to contract — Account taken of studies	Independent teams of discipline engineers (In-house or customer)	Project management also involved. Audit to verify that any non-conformances have been closed out
9 Audit and corrective action	Ensure non-conformances promptly identified and corrective action taken to prevent recurrence	Project management Discipline engineers Quality assurance	Co-ordinate and verify that corrective action completed and that action has been taken to prevent recurrence

Fig. 11.1 — Design control matrix.

Contract review

This is a most important activity but unfortunately insufficient emphasis is given to it in most quality assurance standards. Before any work starts, it is important that all concerned are aware of their responsibilities within the design contract and that they have the right tools with which to perform their job. A review team must therefore be assembled, comprising contract or project management, discipline lead engineers and quality assurance representative.

Work scope
The review team should consider in detail the scope of work and should establish that this is fully understood by all concerned and that the quality plan identifies all the required procedural controls to cover the true scope.

Specifications and standards
It should be ensured that all applicable specifications and standards, of correct issue, are readily available at all activity locations.

Philosophies
These can cover studies, design philosophies—even quality assurance philosophies (where these could be interpreted in different ways). Are these philosophies agreed upon and understood?

Design criteria
Are they all available and understood?

Regulatory requirements
If any regulatory authority is involved regarding safety and/or environmental requirements, then the contract or project team should be aware of all parties involved and the exact nature of the statutory requirements in their current form.

Organisation
Who does what in the contract or project task-force? Who reports to whom and what are each individual's terms of reference? If the organisation is defined and made generally known immediately, then there can be no misconception about reporting responsibilities. A considerable amount of time and misunderstanding can be avoided when the right person to approach concerning any given issue is known.

The same must also be said for the customer's organisation. The customer's representatives who interviewed the project team prior to contract placement need not necessarily be the same people who will be representing the customer on the actual project. In many instances they are not and they may have different ideas and philosophies.

To emphasise the requirements that personnel should be aware of customers' current philosophies, it is worthwhile considering a not uncommon example.

In one such instance, prior to contract placement, discussions duly took place between the quality assurance managers representing the supplier and customer who 'spoke the same language' with regard to quality assurance philosophies.

When the contract was eventually placed, the customer appointed his own project quality assurance manager who had a different approach from that discussed and agreed before contract placement. The philosophies presented by the customer's project quality assurance manager proved to be a 'super-checking' activity, which caused the contractor having either to protest vehemently to the customer and stand his ground or to accept the situation and 'staff-up' the quality assurance group to fulfil the additional responsibilities placed upon him.

As this situation occurred during the halcyon days when most major projects were reimbursed on a basis of time-cost or cost plus rather than lump sum payment, it suited the contractor to take on the additional staff required and to submit a change order to cover the additional costs incurred.

In the long run, neither the customer nor the contractor really benefited from this. The contractor would have made an additional, but unexpected, profit—for which the customer duly paid but it did not increase the contractor's efficiency. In fact, it would have had the opposite effect.

Additionally, the customer suffered because when the time came to let future contracts that same contractor, remembering the previous experience, would build into the bid the cost of the necessary resources to cover a 'super-checking' activity. Other possible bidders, having heard about the experience, would no doubt include a similar contingency cost.

This philosophy can do nothing other than increase what could, in the final analysis, be termed quality costs. The checking activities performed by the project quality assurance department in such a situation should have been carried out by the departments or disciplines actually responsible for undertaking that work.

In this and similar instances, of which there have been many, such costs were not associated with putting things right but with duplicating activities carried out by others. One could ask the question: 'Who eventually benefits from such a philosophy?' In all probability—no one!

Action by quality assurance

The contract review meeting, as for any formal meeting, should be minuted. Minutes of meetings, as for any series of documents, should be produced in a formalised manner. Actions identified during this meeting should be placed on individuals and not departments. These individuals will be named under an action column in the minutes (see Fig. 11.2) for a typical minutes format.

The quality assurance representative should utilise these minutes as a form of check-list and would verify that actions placed on individuals had been dealt with satisfactorily. Where the action remains unresolved, then steps are taken by the quality assurance representative to expedite resolution.

XYZ COMPANY	MINUTES OF MEETING NO.	
Client/Contractor	Project No.	
Place & Date of Meeting	Date typed	
Subject:	Typed by:	
	Page of	
PRESENT	DISTRIBUTION	
ITEM	DESCRIPTION OF DISCUSSION	ACTION BY

XYZ-MAN-007.1

Fig. 11.2 — Minutes.

This type of activity is known as auditing and will be dealt with in much greater detail later.

Document preparation, control and retention

Document preparation is another important activity not given sufficient attention. Documents in this context cover drawings, specifications, data sheets and so on. These should be presented in a correct and uniform manner. Personnel quite often have different ideas on how documents should be formulated. Sometimes ideas developed for previous contracts or projects are used and may not be compatible with current requirements and the rules need to be overhauled. A uniform approach should be agreed, defined and communicated to all concerned before work commences. The customer should be brought into these discussions, since there may be specific contract requirements. For example, the customer may require standard drawings based on A1 sizes and he would be very concerned to find that at the end of a contract the design for which he has paid is presented as a large number of A0 sized drawings, which are too large for existing files and which cause the additional expense of purchasing new filing equipment for which there is no suitable accommodation.

Uniform document presentation helps to avoid errors and facilitates checking, allowing more use of standard checking routines. It is far easier to handle documents when, for example, the contract or project number can always be found in the same corner. It is difficult and time-consuming to check documents whose contents are distributed in different patterns or sequences.

Document identification should be standardised and controlled using logical procedures. Complex numbering systems should be avoided, as these tend to confuse rather than assist in identification and retrieval of documents. The simpler the system the easier it is to operate and control. Numbering systems should, as a minimum, contain the following:

—Contract or project number.
—Document type (denoting whether it is a specification, purchase requisition, design brief, data sheet or drawing).
—Document serial number.
—Document revision status.

The following is a typical arrangement for document identification:

```
                                              8742—S—345—1
     Contract or project number  ─────────────────┘   │   │   │
     Document type  ───────────────────────────────────┘   │   │
     Serial number  ───────────────────────────────────────┘   │
     Revision status  ─────────────────────────────────────────┘
```

Whatever the identification system to be used, the customer will probably require some input and should be consulted before the system is put to use on the contract.

Document approval procedures should be formalised and all those carrying the authority to give approval at each stage (including the customer's representatives) should be named. Specimen sets of initials or signatures should be registered in the appropriate records.

Document checking, including amendments
Checking routines should be formulated. These routines should include as a minimum the types of documents to be checked, the methods of checking and the personnel responsible for checking.

It is important to establish the types of documents to be checked and not make it mandatory for all. In all too many cases has a senior engineer been seen to be furiously appending his signature to a great pile of drawings. All this process involved was for him to lift the bottom right hand corner of each of the drawings in the pile and sign it off as checked. No attention was paid to the content of the drawings and so this 'checking' routine became a meaningless and mechanical exercise.

Why was it done? Because instructions were given that all drawings should be checked regardless of content. A waste of valuable time.

The same principle should apply in the approval of documents. Those which require approval, and by whom the approval is to be given, should be clearly stated. It is as well, also, to specify those which do not require such approval so as to avoid misunderstanding.

The checking and approval of amendments to documents should be similarly formalised.

Document distribution
In these days of readily available (if expensive) photocopying, the sending of copies of all documents to everyone who might conceivably be interested in seeing them is all too common. Such instances are counter-productive and self-defeating. Procedures should, therefore, be established to identify which documents are really needed by selected recipients. Many people may wish to be included on the distribution list whether they need to be or not. Involvement by those who have no need to get involved creates confusion. A matrix chart which lists document types along the left-hand vertical column and has the remaining columns headed with all potential recipients is a useful and concise method for denoting the standard distribution arrangements for project documents. In the matrix, each box will link a document type with a possible addressee, and the matrix will automatically cover all possible permutations. It is simply necessary to leave blank boxes where there is to be no distribution. In each case where documents need to be sent to an addressee, the number of sets to be sent is written in the relevant box. It is stressed again that this should be arranged strictly on a 'need to know' rather than a 'want to know' basis.

A formalised procedure for distribution is also essential to ensure not only that each person who requires documents appears on the list, so that he or she gets them in the first place, but also to ensure that they are in the right quantities (number of sets), of the correct form (e.g. full-sized drawings or microfilms), and that the initial issues are backed up by all revisions.

Retention, retrieval, storage and handover

Details should be documented covering the procedures to be implemented to control document retention, retrieval, storage and handover.

In all probability there will be specific contractual requirments for retention of documents and records generated during the execution of the contract. For example, many sector-based quality assurance schemes demand a limited period for retention of documents. The safety-related industries may be required to retain documents for 25 years or more. Provision should be made to fulfil these requirements.

The longer the retention period the more susceptible the documents will become to damage and/or loss, therefore provision should be made for proper storage and for the method of storage to be adopted. If hard copies are to be retained, then space becomes a major factor, as does the size and type of the containers to be used. The storage problem can be minimised by the use, if approved, of microfilm.

Whatever the retention period and storage methods, there should be a system installed to facilitate ease of retrieval should the need arise—as is very often the case.

On contract completion, if there is a requirement that documents must be handed over to the customer, then the method of handover should be documented.

All these requirements should be considered in the planning stage of a contract or project and not left until documents start to be generated.

Regardless of company size, there is always the need properly to control documentation.

The action by quality assurance would be to verify, initially, the formulation of all necessary procedures to control the document control activity, and to confirm that such procedures have received the required approvals, and subsequently audit to verify the implementation and adherence to the document control system.

Discipline check

A discipline check is carried out to verify the content and accuracy of a document originating from a single engineering discipline. Such checks should be performed by engineers of the appropriate discipline but the checking engineer must not be the same person who carried out the original work. The checker should be of at least the same grade of seniority as the originating engineer. In the case of a one-man discipline (which often occurs on small contracts), it will be necessary to appoint the checker from outside the contract from a corporate department, from another project team or, in the case of extremely critical design, from some qualified third party source.

This type of check not only checks engineering calculations but also the integrity and application of the design. Hence the requirement for the experience qualifications of the engineer carrying out this check to be of, at least, the same level as the originating engineer.

The discipline check procedure should identify the documents which require to be checked and the methods for undertaking the check. One method, for example, would be the issuance of a check print and the checker would identify each satisfactory item in a denoting colour (say green) with queries and/or comments on unsatisfactory or ambiguous conditions in a contrasting colour (say red). The check print would be returned to the originating engineer for action as necessary. This check print should be retained for control purposes. The document, when completed satisfactorily, would be signed by the checker and, when required, by the approval authority.

Before any document is put forward for checking it is in the originating engineer's own interest to verify the quality of his own work by means of a self-check. This should be a fundamental requirement practised by all personnel regardless of discipline.

The action by quality assurance would be again to verify initially the formulation and approval of the required procedure to cover this activity and, subsequently, to audit, as required, to confirm compliance.

Interdiscipline check

Interdiscipline checking assesses not only the content and accuracy of a document but assures compatibility between all the design disciplines involved.

This is an important activity and, if carried out correctly, will minimise manufacturing and installation problems. To give an example, there are many instances in the installation phase of a contract where proper consideration proves not to have been given to the routing of pipework, ducting, cabling and the like, resulting in a great deal of rectification work on site. Liaison between the involved disciplines at the design stage would reduce costs in such instances. It seems obvious that the routing of heating, ventilation and air-condition ducting should be known before concreting takes place on site. Liaison between the HVAC discipline, the architectural and structural disciplines at the design stage is imperative, otherwise it may well become necessary to drill through concrete and steel to accommodate the ducting. Unfortunately, this tends to happen all too often. Such rectification work could have an effect on the integrity of the structural design and may affect safety standards, particularly so if such work is carried out without consulting or liaising with the originating design engineer, as again happens all too frequently.

In the case of an interdiscipline check, a procedure should be developed which would identify which documents would be subjected to such a check, the distribution of the documents and the methods to be adopted when commenting on such documents. The procedure would also identify those responsible for commenting.

Here a document distribution list would be important and it should list all those required to comment on a document. Figs. 11.3, 11.4 and 11.5 are typical examples of such lists. There is also the need to log all documents on an interdiscipline check and Fig. 11.6 shows a typical register. There are various ways of distributing documents for interdiscipline checks.

Parallel issue
This issue, although expeditious, entails considerable copying of documents and requires strict control. The document to be reviewed is issued simultaneously to all interfacing disciplines for their review and comment. The latest date for the return of comments should be indicated and every involved discipline should make comment, even where this means writing 'no comment'. The department responsible for document control should issue the review copies on behalf of the originating discipline, and control and expedite progress to ensure the return of all copies within the latest completion date. Parallel issue is obviously the method best suited where a fast turn-round of documents is required.

Circular issue
As its name implies, this depends upon the circulation of a single issue of the document which is circulated to all interfacing disciplines on a 'round robin' basis. This type of distribution is used where urgency is not the first priority. Care should be taken in arranging the list to include the disciplines required to make comment in order of priority. Here again the department responsible for document control, after issuing the document on behalf of the originating engineer, should expedite and control its progress around the circuit. As for parallel issues, all involved disciplines should make comment.

Flood issue, in conjunction with a review meeting
This is similar to a parallel issue but, instead of inviting comments through the distribution circuit, a meeting is called to review and co-ordinate any such comments. As for any meeting, minutes will be tabled and these will list the comments made for the subsequent attention of the originating discipline. Minutes of meetings are objective evidence of quality and can be used by quality assurance personnel as check-lists for audit purposes.

The action by quality assurance would be as for the previous activities.

Internal design review
At important stages throughout design activities, internal design review meetings should be called to review progress. These meetings will consider all aspects of activities to date. There may be areas of concern, perhaps even updated information from the customer or new legislation concerning such items as safety and certification.

Internal design reviews should be undertaken on a regular basis and should be scheduled at contract commencement. The scheduling of such reviews will be determined by management based upon the duration and

DOCUMENTS PRODUCED BY **Mechanical** DISCIPLINE	ARCHITECTURAL	ELECTRICAL	FIRE & SAFETY	HVAC	INSTRUMENTATION	MECHANICAL	PROCESS	STRUCTURAL	QUALITY ASSURANCE	PROJECT MANAGER	
GENERAL SPECIFICATIONS		√	A			O					
UNIQUE SPECIFICATIONS		√	A			O					
PHILOSOPHIES		√				O				√	
REPORTS		√	A			O				√	
STUDIES		√	A			O				√	
CALCULATIONS	NOT GIVEN AN IDC										
DRAWINGS	√	√	A					√	√		
DATA SHEETS	√	√	A					√			
REQUISITIONS	NOT GIVEN AN IDC										
MECHANICAL EQUIPMENT		√	√			O	A				

IDC   MATRIX MINIMUM DISTRIBUTION
O=   ORIGINATOR
√=   REVIEW
A=   REVIEW AS APPLICABLE

XYZ-ENG-002.1

Fig. 11.3 — IDC matrix.

IDC REVIEW TRANSMITTAL FORM					IDC NO:	
DOCUMENT TITLE: DOCUMENT NO: DISCIPLINE:					REVISION NO:	
IDC REQUESTED BY:					DATE:	
CONTROL DATES			CIRC. ORDER	DISCIPLINE		REVIEWER'S SIGNATURE
TO ACTUAL	FROM REQUIRED	FROM ACTUAL				
				ARCHITECTURAL		
				ELECTRICAL		
				FIRE & SAFETY		
				HVAC		
				INSTRUMENTATION		
				MECHANICAL		
				PROCESS		
				STRUCTURAL		
				QUALITY		
				PROJECT MANAGER		
RETURN 'IDC' COPY TO: REMARKS:						

Fig. 11.4 — IDC matrix.

IDC REVIEW		
REVISION		
DISCIPLINE	SIGNATURE	DATE
ARCHITECTURAL		
ELECTRICAL		
FIRE & SAFETY		
HVAC		
INSTRUMENTATION		
MECHANICAL		
PROCESS		
STRUCTURAL		
QUALITY		
PROJECT MANAGER		

Fig. 11.5 — IDC matrix.

complexity of the contract work scope. Regardless of duration of contract, even if only a few weeks, at least one review should be scheduled.

The methods of scheduling reviews, the people involved, the location and details of such reviews should be subject to procedural controls as with any other activity.

All meetings of this kind should be minuted and any action required assigned to individuals.

The action by quality assurance would be to confirm by audit that any such assigned actions have been satisfactorily dealt with by the person or persons concerned.

Design interface control
Although the design interface control could be linked to the interdiscipline check, it goes far deeper. Design interface control sets out to control the interfaces between systems, contractors, and even regulatory bodies. There are many instances in large projects where more than one design contractor is used, creating not only interfaces between disciplines within one organisation but complex interfaces between the different contractors. The problems encountered in persuading all parties to liaise with one another are enor-

IDC No.	DOCUMENT DETAILS			ORIGINATING DISCIPLINE	DATE IDC COMMENCED	ESTIMATED DATE IDC COMPLETED	DATE IDC COMPLETED	REMARKS
	No.	REV.	TITLE					

INTER-DISCIPLINE CHECK (IDC) REGISTER

XYZ-ENG-002.2

Fig. 11.6 — IDC register.

mous, but not insurmountable. Providing that each of the participating organisations has a compatible design control system, the interface control can work smoothly. A strong customer is needed to set the rules and to get all concerned to keep to them. If different philosophies are allowed to prevail, then interface control can be a great problem.

Methods of interfacing, together with the interface areas, should be clearly defined. The distribution chain for documentation should be directed through a single channel so that definite control is established. In such instances, it is usual to appoint an interface engineer to define the methods and procedures. The customer should be responsible for this activity.

The overall control of this activity, and the responsibility for auditing the interface system, must lie with the customer if this activity is to be effective.

Change control

The control of engineering changes is another very important activity which most quality assurance standards treat much too lightly. It usually receives only a passing mention under the subject of 'document control'. It is generally accepted that many of the major problems arise through the lack of engineering change control, with changes being made to a design without reference to the original design source.

Design changes can emanate from many areas: changes in client requirements, updated information from external sources, new legislation from government bodies relating to safety, environmental matters and the like, and internally from departments within the contracting organisation. All must be documented and they must be subjected to consideration and review in the same systematic manner as the original documents. In addition to aspects of quality, these reviews have to take into account the likely effect of each proposed change on the costs and schedule. Formal procedures for controlling engineering changes will ensure that the customer is always consulted where this is relevant, and a suitably qualified group of people will be selected to give approval to, or reject, each change considered (typically known as a change committee).

Engineering changes could be, in the final analysis, termed document changes, as any change in design will ultimately result in an amendment to design documents. In the author's experience, however, engineering changes should be procedurally controlled separately from ordinary document changes.

The system for control of engineering changes should ensure that such changes, from wherever they originate, are channelled or directed through one recording area, both in and out.

The system should also ensure that all engineering changes are properly documented and receive approval from the responsible person. Responsibilities for authorisation of changes should be identified in the same manner as for the authorisation of the original design.

The level of engineering changes should be also documented. There may be some small changes which could well be authorised by the site manager. Other, more important changes, which could affect the integrity of the design, should be referred back to the original design source for authorisation and approval.

The following are examples of engineering changes which could require alternative procedural controls:

(1) Additions to the contracted scope of work which result in changes to specifications.
(2) Changes to specifications that become necessary to maintain the design integrity.
(3) Changes to specifications that are proposed as desirable to meet new or additional requirements relating to safety, efficiency, cost and schedule, and also those which become necessary to meet customer requirements resulting from market research.
(4) Changes to the original scope of work due to the activities of third party sources which result in excess variations to cost, time and resources.

Whatever the change, it should be controlled and authorised at the appropriate level.

Where changes could affect the activities of others, then engineering change control should ensure that, in such cases, the interfacing disciplines are given the opportunity to comment on them. In other words, they are distributed on an interdiscipline check.

In the case of a change in design to meet customer attitudes—consumer items for example—there should be the means to review the impact of such changes. The department concerned with market research should interface not only with the design department but with sales, finance and production. A change in design to accommodate customer requirements may well prove to be totally uneconomic and difficult to achieve. It is therefore important that the procedures should clearly expose this.

Fig. 11.7 is an example of a typical design modification proposal, which shows the source of the required change and the description of the change (part 1).

At this stage, the decision to proceed or not to proceed further with the change is taken by the responsible person, in this case the project manager (part 2).

If the decision is to proceed, then all involved disciplines estimate the effect of the proposed change on their individual disciplines (part 3).

The effect of the cost in time and resources should be documented and Fig. 11.8 is an example of a typical form which identifies such costs.

Once the impact of the change is calculated, it is then documented in part 4 of the design modification proposal, which is then accepted or rejected by the designated person (part 5).

Should the proposal receive approval by the contractor's management, then it should go forward to the customer for authorisation to proceed. A change in the contract will be required and this should be documented. Fig. 11.9 is a typical example of a design modification request form.

The action by quality assurance would be to verify the formulation and approval of the necessary procedures to control engineering changes and to

XYZ COMPANY	DESIGN MODIFICATION PROPOSAL	PROJECT TITLE PROJECT No. DMP No.

PART 1.
ACTIVITY
ORIGINATOR   DISCIPLINE   DATE

SOURCE OF MODIFICATION PROPOSAL — INDICATE
☐ CLIENT   ☐ XYZ COMPANY   ☐ OTHER

DESCRIPTION OF MODIFICATION (SKETCH, DESCRIPTION
GENERAL INFORMATION, e.g. AFFECTED DOCUMENTS)

PART 2.
THIS MODIFICATION PROPOSAL IS REJECTED/ACCEPTED
FOR FURTHER PROCESSING REASON/AFFECTED
DISCIPLINE

SIGNED..................
PROJECT MANAGER

PART 3.
.........DISCIPLINE. PLEASE ESTIMATE THE EFFECT OF THE ABOVE
PROPOSED MODIFICATION ON YOUR DISCIPLINE

DOCUMENT AFFECTED

☐ FLOW DIAGRAMS	☐ FIRE PROTECTION	☐ CERTIFICATION
☐ P & I.D.	☐ TELECOMS	☐ COMMISSIONING
☐ GA/LAYOUT	☐ OPERATIONS	☐ MAINTENANCE
☐ STRUCT. DRG	☐ STUDIES	☐ FABRICATION
☐ PIPING DRG	☐ REQUISITION	☐ INSTALLATION
☐ INSTR. DRG	☐ SPECIFICATION	☐ HOOK-UP
☐ ELECT. DRG	☐ INTERFACE	☐ HISTOGRAMS
☐ OTHER DRG	☐ WEIGHT	☐ SCHEDULE
☐ VENDOR DRG	☐	☐

PART4.
SUMMARY OF MODIFICATION IMPACT.

SIGNED..................
PROJECT PLANNING ENGINEER

PART 5.
THIS MODIFICATION PROPOSAL IS ACCEPTED/REJECTED.
PREPARE DMR   YES/NO

SIGNED..................
PROJECT MANAGER

XYZ-ENG-003.1

Fig. 11.7 — Design modification proposal.

XYZ COMPANY	SUMMARY OF ADDITIONAL MAN-HOURS & COSTS	PROJECT TITLE
		DMR No.

ENGINEERING & DRAUGHTING HOURS

DISCIPLINE / POSITION	DIRECTOR/ PROJECT MANAGER	SENIOR ENGINEER	ENGINEER	INTERFACE ENGINEER	WEIGHT CONTROL ENGINEER	SENIOR DESIGNER/ CHECKER	DRAUGHTS PERSON	PLANNING ENGINEER	DOCUMENT CONTROLLER	QUALITY ASSURANCE
ARCHITECTURAL										
ELECTRICAL										
FIRE & SAFETY										
INSTRUMENTATION										
INTERFACE CONTROL										
LOSS CONTROL										
MECHANICAL/HVAC										
PROCESS/PIPING										
STRUCTURAL										
QUALITY ASSURANCE										
WEIGHT CONTROL										
ESTIMATED TOTALS										
PROJECT CONTROL										
PURCHASING										
EXPEDITING										
ESTIMATED TOTALS										
ESTIMATED OVERALL MANPOWER COSTS										

SUMMARY OF MODIFICATION COSTS

MANPOWER COSTS		
COMMUNICATIONS		
PRINTING & COMPUTER		
TRAVEL & SUBSISTENCE		
OTHER		
OVERALL TOTAL COSTS		

XYZ-ENG-003.2

Fig. 11.8 — Summary of additional man-hours and costs

XYZ COMPANY	DESIGN MODIFICATION REQUEST	PROJECT TITLE / PROJECT NO:
TO:	DATE:	INITIATOR ☐ CLIENT ☐ CONTRACTOR

TITLE:	PAYMENT ☐ LUMP SUM ☐ REIMBURSABLE ☐ UNIT RATE

CONTRACTOR IS HEREBY INSTRUCTED TO PROCEED
WITH THE WORK DESCRIBED HEREUNDER:

APPLICABLE CORRESPONDENCE

ADJUSTMENT TO CONTRACT:
TOTAL ESTIMATED MAN-HOURS   TOTAL ESTIMATED COST

DOCUMENTS AFFECTED

ESTIMATED IMPACT ON PROGRAMME

WORK TO COMMENCE BY: EFFECT ON CONTRACT SCHEDULE:

PLANNED COMPLETION DATE: EFFECT ON MANNING

ACCEPTED BY CONTRACTOR	APPROVED BY CLIENT
NAME:	NAME:
SIGNATURE:	SIGNATURE:
DATE:	DATE:

XYZ-ENG-003.3

Fig. 11.9 — Design modification request.

monitor, as necessary, such changes through to the designated design source for action, approval and close out.

External design reviews

External design reviews can be carried out either by the contracting company itself, using its own corporate disciplines, or by the customer. The reviews amount to a detailed audit of the design, verifying such items as design adequacy, adherence to contract and the account taken of studies. The timing of these reviews is usually stated in the contract or project schedule, so they should come as a surprise to no one. It is pertinent to pose a number of key questions:

Adequacy of design
Does this accord with the scope of work? This corresponds with the first listed design control, 'contract review'.

Adherence to contract
Has due consideration been given to all contract clauses?

Studies
Has due consideration been given to the results of all field studies which may have been carried out by others?

Engineering management also should be involved in monitoring the results of such a review. All comments and non-conformances should be documented and monitored through to close out and approval.

In addition to the design controls so far described, the terms of the contract, or even the nature of the industry, may call for requirements relating to:

Traceability
Weight and centre of gravity control
Reliability
Criticality
Maintainability
and others

All these should be taken into consideration at the contract review stage and the necessary controls established and implemented.

Traceability control

In cases where traceability of certain materials, components and equipment is required, it will be necessary to implement and operate a system which will trace such materials, components and equipment to their specific source and identify them with their respective material and test certificates.

Traceability, in such instances, should operate throughout the design, manufacture, installation and operational life of the unit.

It should be the responsibility of the relevant design engineer to determine which items require traceability. It is not the quality assurance department's responsibility.

A system for traceability should provide for:

(a) The traceability of materials, components and equipment which may contribute to an accident resulting in loss of life, injury or loss of production.
(b) The establishment, with certainty, of the number and location of all materials, components and equipment items, which, if found to be defective, should be replaced.
(c) The data and information necessary for the preparation of the most efficient maintenance procedures.
(d) The data and information necessary for generating future design modification and improvements.

The extent of traceability to be applied to materials, components and equipment should be specified in the contract documents and should be governed by its application and potential contribution to a safety or loss of production related incident.

The above statement on traceability control would serve as a typical system outline for a quality manual.

The contract review meeting should establish traceability when required and this should be identified in the minutes of the review meeting.

The action by quality assurance should be to verify that traceability requirements have been identified and that the necessary action has been taken to implement such requirements.

To illustrate how traceability could operate, it is worthwhile considering an actual example. A particular contract called up a requirement for a quantity of a special type of relief valve, to be inserted in different locations in the high-pressure system of a major plant.

The relief valve bodies were to be constructed from a very sophisticated material and traceability was required both 'in and out'.

In this case, the requirement would be not only to trace the material in to the supplier through the material certification but to trace the material out again via its heat and cast numbers to other valves which had bodies made from the same batch of material.

This 'in and out' traceability is particularly important in high safety related projects where a number of identical components have been manufactured from the same heat or cast of material.

In the event of failure of one of the components, it would then be necessary to trace the location of all other components which have been manufactured from the same batch in order to take remedial action.

Traceability in such cases demands strict control. Computerisation of the information can ease the burden substantially.

The material certification documentation should identify each valve body with a unique number, together with its specific location in the plant.

Location details should identify the material certification and where it is filed. This, of course, highlights the necessity for the strict control of documentation discussed earlier.

Weight and centre of gravity control
This is a requirement relating particularly to two industries: offshore oil and gas structures; and to certain civil engineering installations. In such cases there are requirements to establish weight limits and to control the weight of equipment and material so as to keep below such limits.

For example, an offshore oil drilling and production platform will operate in a known depth of water. The jacket structure (i.e. the supporting framework for the platform and superstructure) will be designed to support a predetermined topside weight. The total topside weight will be calculated using information obtained from material and equipment suppliers, and others.

Once determined, the weight of the material and equipment should be monitored. This will mean that each specification should include a requirement for each supplier to submit final weights for their item of supply. A continuous monitoring and evaluation system will be required to control this activity effectively.

Any substantial additions to, or reductions in, the total topside weight could have an adverse effect on the integrity of the jacket structure and possibly affect the centre of gravity loadings.

Similarly, the civil engineering industry could have weight control requirements when designing bridges, high-rise developments, multi-storey car parks, and the like.

Reliability
Here again, design controls should be implemented to take into consideration the reliability not only of individual items of material and equipment but also complete plants. If, for example, a power generation unit is required to operate at a given level for 90% of its working life, then a detailed review of all components should be undertaken to evaluate their capability to meet such reliability requirements. The criticality of each item would therefore need to be defined.

Criticality
Many customers are now looking at the criticality of materiel, in order to establish the level of inspection or tests required to 'prove' the item.

Criticality can be related to safety or loss of production and it determines, in effect, the weakest link in a chain.

Many attempts have been made to establish a formula to determine criticality levels but none has been completely effective as there are so many variables to be considered, such as:

The complexity of design
The complexity of production
The complexity of maintenance
Safety requirements
Ecological and environmental hazards
Monetary investment

All of these must be equated against the reliability requirement of the total plant.

In many instances the criticality of materiel has been left to the judgement of the individual design engineer but this has resulted in 'overkill', as most engineers consider their own equipment to be the most important and demand all sorts of inspection and tests to prove it. Not enough consideration has been given to the use of tried and tested components and the avoidance of tight tolerances which are difficult, if not impossible to achieve, during production. Lack of discipline checking aggravates the problem. The end result has been to inspect everything regardless of its end use.

The use of criticality determination is, therefore, a logical step in the reduction of unnecessary inspection. Whatever the methods used, the end result can only be effective and economical.

As an example, consider a pump. A customer orders two identical pumps to a known specification. One of these pumps is to be used in a fire-fighting situation; the other in a waste water disposal situation. It stands to reason that the fire pump is therefore more 'critical' in its application than the other pump. The customer may, therefore, feel that he needs to attend the testing of the fire pump and should possibly highlight this in the contract.

Maintainability

This goes hand in hand with reliability. The maintenance requirements of a unit should be determined. For example, a power generation unit may be required to operate continuously, in which case, in order to achieve what is in effect 100% reliability, it will probably be necessary to include a back-up unit, and the installation of two units side by side. The location of these units, if placed too close together, could hamper the activities of maintenance crews. The location of vital components, if badly located, could result in unnecessary dismantling work to carry out a simple maintenance task.

It is a matter of common experience that many major maintenance problems have occurred due to lack of attention in this area. Indeed this matter of maintainability is of very wide application. Motor cars, for example, are usually better in this respect than they used to be, although still leaving much to be desired. In the case of a home appliance, such as a vacuum cleaner, there are instances where, on some models, it is necessary virtually to dismantle the complete machine to change the brush drive band. Lack of consideration to such maintenance details is all too common.

The action by the quality assurance in all these instances would be to verify, initially, the establishment of procedures to control these activities and then to monitor, by audit, their implementation. effectiveness and adherence.

It is unfortunate that, in many industries, the responsibilities for undertaking the actual activities for traceability, weight control, reliability and maintainability are placed upon the quality assurance department.

These activities are 'safety' related and, as safety and quality are regarded as synonymous, the philosophy in such cases is that the quality department must therefore be responsible. This is rather a short-sighted policy, as the result can be neither productive nor cost-effective. Traceability, reliability and maintainability are engineering matters and should be dealt with by engineers. The quality assurance department would verify that all such activities have been carried out in accordance with requirements.

Audit and corrective action

It is most unlikely that the design activities will be completed without some corrective action becoming necessary. This is where the quality assurance department requires the support of senior management. Without it, they would not have the authority to carry through their job. All non-conformances identified during the checks and audits already described, whether discovered by the quality assurance staff or by the engineers themselves, should be dealt with immediately and steps taken to prevent their recurrence.

Where a non-conformance is identified, but the corrective action taken by the department responsible is considered to be insufficient to prevent repetition, then the quality assurance representative must be able to call upon support from management in order that the problem can be resolved effectively. The intention of design control is to ensure that the eventual design meets all customer and regulatory requirements. At the completion of this activity, the design will result in the commitment of expensive resources to produce the hardware. It is therefore essential that the audits carried out by the quality assurance representative are taken seriously and their results acted upon.

SYSTEMS OUTLINES

In Figs. 11.10 and 11.11 the activities of contract review (planning) and engineering change control have been reduced into a form which could, if they are applicable, be used as system outlines in a quality manual. These outlines are in addition to those for traceability, which was referred to earlier, and for design control detailed in Fig. 4.2.

The next act in the total presentation is to ensure that the purchasing of the hardware and the associated services is controlled in the same systematic manner as the design.

Typical system outline for contract review

1.0 Prior to commencement of any work, provision shall be made for a detailed review of all contract documents.

    1.1 This review shall confirm the following criteria:

        – Work scope
        – Client specifications
        – Client philosophies
        – Regulatory requirements
        – Relevant national and XYZ Company standards and procedures

    1.2 As a result of the review, should any of the above items require clarification or amplification, the XYZ Company Contract Manager shall inform the customer and maintain an Action Log until the queries are satisfactorily resolved.

    1.3 Following the review of contract requirements, all assigned lead personnel shall prepare a statement of all criteria for their discipline prior to the start of project (contract) activities. In the case of one-man disciplines, the statement shall be prepared by that person.

    1.4 Each statement shall contain details of the work scope and lists of the specific applicable customer specifications and philosophies, regulatory requirements and national and XYZ Company standards and procedures.

    1.5 The XYZ Company Contract Manager shall ensure the criteria from each discipline meet the requirements of the contract.

    1.6 It shall be the responsibility of XYZ Company Management to ensure that all the documents referred to in Section 1.1 are maintained up to date in the Document Control Centre with adequate copies to enable them to be accessible to all relevant personnel.

    1.7 Each department and/or discipline shall maintain a file of, or have access to, each of the referenced documents in section 1.1 which are applicable to their scope of work.

    1.8 Details of WHO, WHAT and HOW are defined in XYZ Company written procedures and work instructions.

Fig. 11.10 — Typical system outline for contract review.

Typical system outline for engineering change control

1.0 The XYZ Company Engineering Department shall implement and operate a system which shall control changes from wherever they originate and which shall ensure they are channelled through one recording area both in and out.

    1.1 The system shall also ensure that all changes are correctly documented and have received authorisation from the original design source to be actioned.

    1.2 Where design interfaces were involved in the original design, then changes to such design shall include a review by the interfacing disciplines.

    1.3 Engineering change control shall provide for four categories of change as follows:

        1.3.1 Category 1 which is an addition to the contracted scope of work and which results in changes to the specifications.

        1.3.2 Category 2 are changes to specifications that become necessary to maintain the design integrity.

        1.3.3 Category 3 are changes to specifications that are proposed as desirable to meet new or additional requirements relating to safety, efficiency, cost and schedule, and also those which become necessary to meet customer requirements resulting from market research.

        1.3.4 Category 4 are changes to the original scope of work due to the activities of third party sources which result in excess variations to cost, time and resources.

    1.4 Details of WHO, WHAT and HOW shall be defined in XYZ Company written procedures and work instructions.

Fig. 11.11 — Typical system outline for engineering change control.

12

Procurement control

Regardless of the industry with which an organisation is concerned, there will always be the need to purchase items and/or services of some sort or another. The control over these activities therefore is most important if one is to obtain value for money plus on-time delivery. All the quality assurance programme standards, at all levels, stress the requirement for adequate controls in this area.

Referring back to Fig. 4.4 'Quality assurance in making a cake', it is to be noticed that even the person concerned with cake-making goes through a verification of purchasing sources. Not only does the cook know the type and make or brand of the ingredients which enhance the finished cake, but he or she invariably knows the cheapest source of supply. Although this information is not actually documented as it would be in a formalised quality assurance programme, nevertheless an assessment of procurement sources has been effectively carried out.

Similarly in industry, be it a hardware-related or a service industry, there should be some system for evaluating procurement sources.

THE MAJOR ACTIVITIES

As for design control, those activities considered to be the most important in the procurement activity have been compiled for ease of reference into a tabulated form, Fig. 12.1. The table carries the same headings:

— Activity
— Scope
— Performed by
— Action by quality assurance

Each activity will be dealt with in a similar manner.

Master inspection and test check-list

As mentioned during the formulation of the inspection and test plan, there may be instances where the customer (in this case the purchaser) imposes certain inspection and test requirements upon the supplier to 'prove' that an item meets certain additional safety or critical conditions. In such cases, it is

PROCUREMENT CONTROL

ACTIVITY	SCOPE	PERFORMED BY	ACTION BY QA
1 Master inspection and test check-list (MITCL)	Establish and document: Equipment criticality Inspection check-points NDT requirements Acceptance tests Certification Weight control Traceability	Design engineers Quality control department	Verify issue and approval of MITCL
2 Approve suppliers for bid list (if not previously approved)	Assess suppliers for acceptability in: Engineering Quality Economics/schedule Financial stability	Discipline engineers Purchasing department Quality assurance	Assess the implementation and effectiveness of supplier's quality programme and compare MITCL with supplier's in-house controls
3 Tender package development and issue	Collate all documents/specifications/drawings/MITCL etc. and submit to approved bidders	Puchasing department Discipline engineers Quality assurance	Review, as required, tender packages for completeness
4 Bid package review	Review bid packages for: Engineering Schedule Economics Quality	Contract management Discipline engineers Purchasing department Quality assurance	Monitor, as required, bid reviews to the acceptance of one supplier
5 Pre-award meeting	Review with approved supplier(s) the contract requirements including inspection and test	Contract management Discipline engineers Purchasing department Quality control department Quality assurance	Verify supplier's intended compliance with contract requirements. Establish audit schedule and confirm inspection and test plan
6 Contract award	Collate all documents/specifications/drawings/final inspection and test plan and issue to approved supplier(s)	Purchasing department Quality assurance	Review, as required, contract documents for completeness
7 **Post-award meeting**	Review and confirm with supplier(s): Inspection requirements Certification requirements Hold points Test programme	Quality control personnel Quality assurance	Verify supplier's compliance with requirements. Finalise QA audit schedule
8 Supplier surveillance	Issue relevant sections of contract to quality control personnel and: Review inspection details Confirm certification/documentation requirements Reporting requirements	Quality control personnel	Monitor supplier's performance with own quality plan. Verify QC personnel compliance with inspection and test plan
9 Audit and corrective action	Ensure non-comformances promptly identified and corrective action taken to prevent recurrence	Contract management Supplier's management Quality assurance	Co-ordinate and verify that corrective action completed and that action has been taken to prevent recurrence

Fig. 12.1 — Procurement matrix.

recommended that the customer or purchaser develops his own inspection and test plan for inclusion in the tender documents. In such instances, this document could be termed a master inspection and test check-list to differentiate it from the supplier's own document.

This master check-list should identify all the inspection check points relevant to the criticality of the materiel; it should also list requirements for non-destructive testing, acceptance testing, certification and documentation.

This master inspection and test check-list is, as has already been established, basically a schedule of inspection and test points which the customer would expect the potential supplier to include within his own quality control system for the contracted materiel. It becomes a guideline which sets out the minimum requirements for control and surveillance.

Where weight control is a requirement, then methods of reporting weights should be included. Similarly, traceability of items or batches should also be included, if required.

The master inspection and test check-list is not considered to be a mandatory exercise but its development is recommended if only as a check to place the criticality of materiel at the right level. The customer's own quality control department should have an input into this document as that department would be concerned with its administration after contract award. The quality control department should also review the requirements for 'inspectability and testability'. For example, some configurations of a fabricated item may not lend themselves to certain methods of non-destructive testing. Only those continuously involved in non-destructive testing would be aware of the associated problems.

In other words, the supplier should not be expected to perform tests which are difficult to achieve and the results of which might be worthless. The supplier will, no doubt, be happy to produce test pieces, at a price!

Unfortunately, it is all too common in practice to seek to impose unnecessary tolerances and test requirements on suppliers which may, indeed, be impossible to meet. The supplier, for his part, is not always blameless, as very often he will accept a contract knowing full well that he will be unable to comply with all requirements.

The action by quality assurance should be to verify that the master inspection and test check-list has been developed where required and that all interfacing disciplines, including the quality control department, have reviewed and commented on it and that all comments have been satisfactorily closed out. Approval of the document by the correct approval authority should be also verified.

The master inspection and test check-list will form part of the tender package, together with specifications, drawings, data sheets, contract conditions, quality assurance requirements, and so on.

Approve suppliers for bid list
Before a tender package can be issued, it will be necessary to establish who is to tender for the materiel or services. In all probability, there will be a

number of potential suppliers but, if there is no previous history of a supplier on record, then it would be prudent to assess that potential supplier's capability.

The assessment of a supplier can take many forms. A history of a supplier's capability can be established purely on a quality/delivery record. Where such a supplier makes frequent and regular deliveries to a customer, then confidence is established and maintained on a continuing basis. This method of assessment should be documented and updated by delivery analyses.

In other instances, one could verify a supplier's capability either by inspecting the materiel at the supplier's premises before delivery or by incoming inspection on receipt. Although effective this may not be very economical when materiel is rejected. This method of assessment should also be documented and updated by inspection results.

The responsibility for quality should lie with the supplier and it should not be necessary for the customer to 'inspect' quality into supplied items.

There are a number of countries—UK, Canada, Australia and others- —which operate assessment programmes. Assessments are carried out by accredited bodies to the appropriate national quality assurance standard and successful companies are registered accordingly and are entered in a buyers' guide.

If an organisation uses such a buyers' guide as an assessment source, then this method should be similarly documented.

In the cases of very complex plant or equipment, such methods of assessment would not be very meaningful, particularly if additional quality requirements are to be stipulated. It will be necessary, therefore, particularly when the firm is unknown, to carry out an assessment to verify whether or not the potential supplier is capable of meeting not only quality requirements but engineering, delivery and economic requirements.

An assessment, therefore, falls into four distinct parts:

— Engineering
— Quality
— Economics/schedule
— Financial stability

Engineering

An evaluation should be made of the potential supplier's manufacturing facilities to verify whether he has the capability to manufacture or supply the materials/equipment to the specification.

A study of his fulfilment of recent contracts of comparable size and complexity should also be undertaken, as this would assist in substantiating his capabilities.

As this part of the assessment relates to the manufacturing capabilities, it should be carried out by personnel who are familiar with production activities, i.e. qualified engineers.

Quality

An evaluation should be made of the potential supplier's own quality programme. This should be documented in the form of a quality manual and the evaluation would verify whether his quality programme is being effectively implemented and receives the full support of senior management.

At this stage, with no contract made, there is nothing binding upon a potential supplier to conform to any given requirement. It is possible only to review the quality programme and to make observations on any apparent deficiency; perhaps advising the supplier that the deficiency, if not rectified, could have an adverse effect on contract award.

The customer's own quality assurance personnel would be responsible for this activity.

Economics/schedule

An evaluation should be made of the potential supplier's prices and delivery record. Have his prices for similar contracts been competitive and is there a proven ability to deliver on time?

Financial stability

An evaluation should be made of the potential supplier's financial stability, particularly where high-cost, long-delivery contracts are concerned. In times of recession, it is not uncommon for companies to go into receivership. If this should happen, then there is no knowing what effect this could have on contracts already half-completed (possibly after considerable advance progress payments have been committed—and perhaps lost irrevocably). It is often prudent therefore to examine the supplier's published accounts or seek a report from an accredited agency.

The last two items would be evaluated probably by the customer's contracts department.

During the assessment, a comparison could be made between the supplier's own inspection and test plans for recent orders of comparable size and complexity and the master inspection and test check-list. This comparison should verify whether the supplier does take into consideration, during the planning stage, any unique customer requirements for inspection and testing, and whether mandatory hold points are documented and adhered to.

The results of the assessment should be evaluated by all parties involved, resulting in an agreement to approve or disapprove the supplier. In the case of approval, the supplier would then be entered on the bidders' list.

Methods of carrying out assessments and methods used in evaluating results should be procedurally controlled.

Tender package development and issue

During the assessment period, possibly even earlier, tender packages will have been assembled. These will comprise the specifications, drawings, data sheets, delivery requirements, inspection and test plans, and so on, which together define the commitment which the supplier is being invited to undertake. Although the purchasing department should compile and issue the tender package, both the engineering and quality assurance departments should be involved. The tender package is, in effect, subjected to an interdiscipline check as in design control. Thus the tender package should receive a review for completeness and accuracy. It should then be issued to approved potential suppliers.

Again, as for any series of documents, tender packages should follow a uniform presentation with a standard index. This means, of course, that there will be a requirement for a procedure, which should establish the methods for development and issue of such packages.

The action by quality assurance should be to verify, as required to establish confidence, that tender packages have been developed, approved and issued in accordance with procedure and that all appropriate documents, specifications, drawings and quality requirements are included and that the packages were issued to the agreed and approved bidders.

Bid package review

When all tenders from suppliers have been received, they should be reviewed for engineering content, quality, price and delivery.

Engineering department should review the tenderers' proposals for supply. There may be cases where a supplier proposes alternative methods, materials or equipment from those listed in the specification, and the engineering department should comment on this, stating whether or not the changes represent improvements or otherwise, and whether or not they are acceptable. The purchasing department should consider the price and delivery proposals. When the potential sources of supply are remote from the sites where goods are to be delivered, especially where overseas transport and international boundaries are involved, it is necessary to consider not just the ex-works price quoted but the total cost of purchase, transport, insurance, duties and taxes payable to obtain an on-site cost. The quality assurance department should review the package for compliance with the quality programme level, quality acceptance criteria, inspection and test plan and certification.

Bid summary

When a choice has to be made between a number of suppliers, it is of benefit to tabulate the main points arising from the review on a bid summary sheet. This is arranged to display the various price and delivery promises, all translated to a common set of units for easy and meaningful comparison. For example, all the costs converted to one monetary system: US dollars, pounds sterling.

Tabulations are less useful for technical and quality comments, being too limited in space, but they can be used for brief comments, especially where such comments give a definitive preference or rejection. Final choice of supplier is often a complex affair, involving the company's quality, technical and commercial departments.

All too often, unfortunately, the 'bottom line' is the deciding factor and the contract is awarded to the lowest bidder. The fact that the lowest bidder may have a poor quality system is not given sufficient weighting, with the end result that the customer may well find himself in the position of having to decide between quality and delivery. There is much truth in that well-known saying.

> The bitterness of poor quality remains long after the sweetness of low price is forgotten.

It is necessary, therefore, for the views of the quality assurance department to be taken into account in the selection of the actual supply source, together with those of the engineering and purchasing departments. This again serves to emphasise the importance of the quality assurance department within the organisation.

Having reviewed the bid packages in their own right, the *action by quality assurance* will be to verify that all comments made by others have been considered and actioned, thus leading to the acceptance of one supplier (or more as the case may be, depending on the scope of supply).

Having identified this supplier, in the case of large or highly critical items and prior to the issue of a formal contract or purchase order, it is prudent to call in that supplier to attend what is usually termed a pre-award meeting.

Pre-award meeting

Pre-award meetings with the selected suppliers are held to review jointly the contract requirements and to obtain the suppliers' understanding and agreement. Such meetings correspond to the contract review meetings discussed in design control.

A quality assurance representative must be present at this meeting—this is most important! Experience has shown that this is one meeting where the quality assurance department involvement is often overlooked and any quality problems encountered at this meeting tend to be swept aside in the desire to place the order and commence production. This is where the 'we didn't have time' syndrome first manifests itself, resulting in much greater problems further down the line with the subsequent high cost of rectification.

A procedure should be developed which indicates where and how such a meeting is to be arranged, who is to organise and chair it and who is to attend. Quality assurance should, in all circumstances, be invited to attend such meetings. It is at the discretion of the quality assurance representative, and not others, to determine whether or not it is necessary to attend.

Each pre-award meeting will verify the supplier's intended compliance with the contract and will also take into account quality programme deficiencies observed when the supplier was assessed before the issue of the bid package. Items identified on the master inspection and test check-list should be reviewed against the supplier's own inspection and test plan, and this comparison will confirm whether or not the customer will need to exercise any quality control activities himself. Any contentious issues should be resolved at this meeting, or at least very shortly afterwards. Ambiguities and unresolved problems could result in delays or additional costs later on.

The quality assurance representative may at this time establish an interim audit schedule, although this is a little difficult to do until the supplier has produced his project quality plan for approval, which, as for the design control element, should be established in accordance with tender document requirements.

The pre-award meeting should be minuted and any actions required assigned to individuals. It should be recognised that an interface problem may arise as two organisations are involved—the customer and the supplier.

It should be the responsibility of the customer's quality assurance department to verify by audit that any assigned customer actions have been closed out. The verification of close-out of supplier-assigned actions should be the responsibility of the supplier's own quality assurance department. Both the customer's and the supplier's quality assurance departments should liaise to establish total conformance.

All verification activities should be documented.

Contract award

The purchase order or contract package issue, apart from being issued only to the chosen supplier(s), should be treated in the same way as the invitation to tender documents. Again, it involves the interdiscipline check and review to verify completeness, accuracy and compliance with any agreements arising from the pre-award meeting.

The action by quality assurance should be to verify—as required to establish confidence—that contract documents have been developed, approved and issued in accordance with procedure and that all comments resulting from the pre-award meeting have been taken into consideration.

Post-award meeting

Among the scheduled dates proposed in the tender documents and firmed up in the issued contract should be the date by which the supplier is expected to present the customer with his quality plan. About seven days after receipt of the quality plan, it should be reviewed between customer and supplier in a post-award meeting. An audit schedule can be agreed at the same time, together with inspection hold points, certification and other documentation requirements, and the test programme. The audit schedule should make provision for an initial system audit to confirm quality plan awareness, with subsequent compliance audits arranged to cover weak or possible non-conforming areas exposed during the original supplier assessment. In addition to any audits undertaken by the customer, the supplier should verify, also by audit, that his own quality programme is being effectively implemented.

Attendance at this meeting is usually limited to quality assurance and quality control personnel of both customer and supplier.

Supplier surveillance

Once manufacture is under way, the supplier's own quality control department should be verifying by inspection and/or surveillance that each activity in the production cycle is correct to specification and objective evidence evaluated to confirm this.

Additionally, the supplier's own quality assurance department should be verifying, by internal audit, that all activities related to the quality plan, including production and quality control, are effective.

The customer's own quality control department should limit their involvement to verifying that specific inspections and tests required by contract are carried out correctly and at the right time, and that there is objective evidence to substantiate this, i.e. test reports, certificates.

Audit and corrective action

The customer's quality assurance activities are threefold:

(1) To verify, initially, the establishment of procedures to control the customer's own procurement activities and then to monitor, by audit, their implementation, adherence and effectiveness.
(2) To verify the establishment by the supplier of a quality plan and then to monitor by audit the implementaion and effectiveness of, and adherence to, the plan.
(3) To verify the establishment of both the master inspection and test checklist and the supplier's inspection and test plan, and to monitor, by audit, the activities of quality control personnel in the implementation of the inspection and test plan.

All non-conformances exposed during these three activities would be addressed by corrective action requests upon the appropriate party, with follow-up action to verify that corrective action has been taken and steps taken to prevent a recurrence of the deficiency.

SERVICE CONTRACTS

Most of the activities described in this chapter have been centred around the procurement of hardware. It should be borne in mind that the procurement of services (people-related industries) should also follow the same pattern.

Companies offering services should also be evaluated in the same manner as those manufacturing and supplying materiel.

The companies would be assessed to confirm acceptability of the services they offer, that the personnel carrying out the services are suitably qualified and experienced and that the service can be completed on time and within budget.

Tender package development would apply, as would bid package review.

A pre-award meeting would be also a requirement where applicable.

A service contract award would be controlled in the same manner as a contract award for a manufactured item.

The post-award meeting could also be applicable.

The monitoring, by the customer, of personnel fulfilling a service contract would, in all probability, be part of the contract requirements. Particularly so in the case of personnel 'bought-in' to perform a given task: draughting, office cleaning, security, and the like.

Audit and corrective action would be equally applicable.

The requirement, therefore, of all quality assurance standards is that control of procurement should cover both materiel and services.

SYSTEM OUTLINE

The activities thus detailed in procurement control can now be condensed into a systems outline. This outline is given in Fig. 12.2 and could be used in a quality manual to describe what a company does to control purchased materiel and services.

The contract has now been placed and manufacture is about to commence. The next act is manufacturing control.

Typical system outline for control of purchased materiel and services

---

1.0 The XYZ Company shall implement and operate a system which shall provide for the control of materiel and/or services purchased for in-house use or for use on contracts or projects.

    1.1 The XYZ Company Purchasing Department shall be responsible for the implementation of the system which shall involve, as required, other interfacing departments or disciplines.

    1.2 All sources of supply shall be evaluated and approved prior to placing them on the acceptable suppliers list.

    1.3 Evaluation and approval of suppliers shall be determined by all or any of the following methods, depending on the nature and extent of the materiel or services to be supplied:

        1.3.1 Assessment at the supplier's premises to verify quality, production, delivery and price.

        1.3.2 Use of third party approval services, such as a recognised and accredited assessment body associated with a buyer's guide.

        1.3.3 Continual verification by in-process or incoming inspection.

    1.4 A current list of all acceptable suppliers shall be kept up to date and distributed, as required, by the Purchasing Department. Distribution of such lists shall be under controlled conditions.

    1.5 It shall be the responsibility of the Purchasing Department to verify that the relevant suppliers are in possession of all the applicable data required to supply the contracted materiel and services.

    1.6 Contract documents shall be monitored, as required, by the Quality Assurance Department to verify that all such relevant information applicable to the materiel and services is included.

/2....

Fig. 12.2 — Typical system outline for control of purchased materiel and services.

1.7 Where required by contract, all data relevant to the supply of materiel and services shall be made available for customer's review.

1.8 Where any of the following conditions exist, the XYZ Company Quality Control Deparment shall verify, by inspection at the supplier's premises, compliance with requirements:

    1.8.1 Where compliance with requirements cannot be verified during subsequent production activities or where destructive testing is necessary.

    1.8.2 Where special processes, including intermediate testing, is required.

    1.8.3 Where verification of compliance during later stages would require the replacement of high-cost preservation and packaging materials.

    1.8.4 Where materiel is to be shipped to a destination other than the XYZ Company.

1.9 Amendments to contract documents shall be processed in the same manner as the original documents. Traceability of all amendments to the original contract shall be maintained at all times.

1.10 Details of WHO, WHAT and HOW are defined in XYZ Company written procedures and work instructions.

Fig. 12.2a

13

Manufacturing and services control

Manufacturing control is a function which is given a great deal of prominence in all quality assurance standards. It is a function which relates directly to the hardware and it is the hardware which customers use as the yardstick to measure quality.

FITNESS FOR PURPOSE

The production of hardware in a fit for purpose conditon is, therefore, considered to be in the majority of instances the sole criterion of a quality assurance scheme. While such a philosophy is admirable, it does not unfortunately take into consideration the efficiency and effectiveness of all the other functions which are directly or indirectly connected with the manufactured item and leading subsequently to customer satisfaction. The control of manufacture should be considered, therefore, as only a part of the total presentation and should not overpower, or be subservient to, any other controls.

Manufacturers, in the main, do supply items fit for purpose, but, in some instances, because of the high cost involved in achieving the fit for purpose condition due to ineffective control, many manufacturers become uncompetitive and gradually lose their share of the market. This loss of market share leads to a massive reappraisal of a company's position, usually resulting in a reduction of the work-force. If the company concerned has no real means of locating the problem area, due to lack of a documented quality programme, there is no means of 'measuring' the effectiveness of the manufacturing process, or any other process for that matter. The end result, in such a situation, may well be to reduce the 'overhead' staff as they are considered not to be contributing to the fit for purpose condition of the hardware.

It is important, therefore, that all activities and functions of an organisation should be controlled, including manufacture, but not to the detriment of other functions such as administration, sales, marketing, maintenance, installation and after-sales service.

There are many companies that do not manufacture a hardware product: they offer a service, such as insurance, banking, security, office cleaning, and so on. These companies must also consider the control of the service(s) which they offer. The services rendered must totally satisfy the customer just as a manufactured item must also totally satisfy the customer.

It has been stated by many service organisations that quality assurance standards are related to design and manufacturing only and cannot be used in a service environment. This is most certainly not the case, as has been partially shown in procurement control. The majority of 'manufacturing' controls apply equally as well to services.

THE MAJOR ACTIVITIES

As for both design and procurement control, the activities considered to be the most important in manufacturing have been compiled into a tabulated form (Fig. 13.1). In this instance, however, additional columns have been added to show a service scope and performance which will identify how the controls used in manufacturing relate equally to service organisations.

As previously, each activity is dealt with in detail.

Contract review (planning)

As has been discussed, a system to review customer requirements and to plan for the contract or project execution is most important. It should be carried out regardless of the size or nature of the contract. Even a very small company, when receiving an order from a customer, usually carries out a contract review activity, without perhaps recognising it as such, by reading the order and then determining what actions, equipment, materials, and so on, are required to fulfil the order. In many instances, however, this activity is not documented but it occurs just the same. The larger organisation, where numbers of staff are involved, should document the contract review activity, in order that the necessary co-ordination, liaison and understanding of contract requirements can be achieved and can be seen to have been achieved.

The manufacture of an item, or the execution of a service, as for design, should include such an activity and this should be undertaken before any work commences. All concerned should be aware of their responsibilities and a review team should be assembled to review the contract and to plan its execution.

Work scope

The review should entail a detailed consideration of the scope of work and a verification that the scope is fully understood by all concerned.

A manufacturing organisation should then consider:

MANUFACTURING & SERVICES CONTROL

ACTIVITY	SCOPE-MANUFACTURING	PERFORMED BY	SCOPE-SERVICES	PERFORMED BY	ACTION BY QA
1 Contract review	Review work scope Specifications and standards Material requirements Inspection and test requirements Manufacturing processes Organisation	Management Production Quality assurance	Review work scope Customer requirements Staffing levels and experience Organisation	Management Service departments Quality assurance	Verify that missing or ambiguous information has been followed up and satisfactorily closed out by the responsible person
2 Document preparation control and retention	Ensure correct and uniform presentation of documents. Ensure formal preparation, identification, checking, approval and distribution, including amendments. Verify retention, retrieval, storage and handover requirements	Management Production Quality control	Ensure correct and uniform presentation of documents. Ensure formal preparation, identification, checking, approval and distribution, including amendments. Verify retention, retrieval, storage and handover requirements	Management Service department	Audit adherence to procedure
3 Control of inspection Measuring and test equipment	Verify: Equipment to be controlled Standards for control Calibration method Calibration interval Identification of calibration status	Management Production	Verify: Equipment to be controlled Standards for control Equipment status Servicing interval	Management Appropriate department	Audit adherence to procedure
4 Control of purchased materiel and services	Assure methods of adequately assessing supplier's ability to meet contract requirements	Purchasing department Production Quality control Quality assurance	Assure methods of adequately assessing supplier's ability to meet contract requirements	Purchasing department User department Quality assurance	Audit adherence to procedure as required.
5 Incoming inspection	Verify: Materiel conformity to requirements	Quality control	Verify that purchased items conform to requirements	Purchasing department	Audit adherence to inspection and test plan (work routines)
6 Purchaser-supplied materiel (where applicable)	Verify: Type, condition and quantity on receipt Identify and separate from own materiel	Quality control	Verify type, condition and quantity on receipt. Identify	Contract department	Audit adherence to inspection and test plan (work routines)

Fig. 13.1 — Manufacturing and services matrix.

MANUFACTURING & SERVICES CONTROL

ACTIVITY	SCOPE-MANUFACTURING	PERFORMED BY	SCOPE-SERVICES	PERFORMED BY	ACTION BY QA
7 In-process inspection	Verify adherence to specification during manufacture by inspection and/or test. Identification. Documentation	Quality control	Verify adherence to requirements during the service activity	Supervisory staff	Audit adherence to inspection and test plan (work routines).
8 Final inspection	Verify adherence to specification on completion by inspection and/or test. Identification. Documentation	Quality control	Verify adherence to requirements on service completion. Identification. Documentation	Supervisory staff	Audit adherence to inspection and test plan (work routines).
9 Sampling (where applicable)	Verify use of sampling schemes. Methods. Standards	Quality control	Verify use of sampling schemes	Supervisory staff	Audit adherence to inspection and test plan (work routines).
10 Inspection status	Verify methods of indicating inspection status for: Awaiting inspection Inspected accepted Inspected and rejected	Quality control	Verify methods of indicating action status for: Awaiting action Actioned and accepted Actioned and rejected	Supervisory staff	Audit adherence to procedure.
11 Identification and traceability (where applicable)	Verify requirements for traceability of material. Identification Documentation	Production Quality control	Not applicable	Not applicable	Audit adherence to inspection and test plan.
12 Handling and storage	Verify handling and storage methods.	Production Quality control	Verify handling and storage methods	Supervisory staff	Audit adherence to inspection and test plan (work routines).

Fig. 13.1 — Manufacturing and services matrix.

MANUFACTURING & SERVICES CONTROL

ACTIVITY	SCOPE-MANUFACTURING	PERFORMED BY	SCOPE-SERVICES	PERFORMED BY	ACTION BY QA
13 Special processes	Verify which manufacturing processes fall into the special category. Determine methods of control, maintenance and calibration of special process equipment. Suitability of personnel performing special processes	Production Quality control	Verify which processes fall into the special category. Determine methods of control. Maintenance of special process equipment. Suitability of personnel performing special processes.	Supervisory staff	Audit adherence to procedure
14 Preservation, packaging and shipping	Verify requirements and availability of materiel, processes and equipment	Production Purchasing Quality control	Verify requirements and availability of material and resources	Supervisory staff	Audit adherence to inspection and test plan (work routines)
15 Non-conforming items	Verify methods of identifying and dispositioning non-conforming items	Production Quality control	Verify methods of identifying and correcting non-conforming or unacceptable services	Management Appropriate department	Audit adherence to procedure
16 Records	Verify: Requirements Format Contents Storage Retrieval Retention period	Library Document control centre	Verify: Requirements Format Contents Storage Retrieval Retention period	Library Document control centre	Audit adherence to procedure
17 Training	Verify and document training needs. Methods. Records	Management Department heads	Verify and document training needs. Methods. Records	Management Department heads	Audit adherence to procedure
18 Audit and corrective action	Ensure non-conformances promptly identified and corrective action taken to prevent recurrence	Management Quality assurance	Ensure non-conformances promptly identified and corrective action taken to prevent recurrence	Management Department heads	Audit adherence to procedure

Fig. 13.1 — Manufacturing and services matrix.

Specifications and Standards
It should be established that all applicable specifications and standards of correct issue are readily available at all activity locations.

Material requirements
It should be ensured that the correct materials, in the right sizes and quantities, are available. Where materials have to be ordered, then the sources of such materials should be assessed together with delivery, price and quality. The actual mechanics of this activity would be covered by the control of purchased materiel and services.

Inspection and test requirements
If any special inspections or tests are required by contract, or if any regulatory body is involved, then the review team should be aware of these and should schedule the requirements into their own inspection and test plan. Specialised testing equipment may have to be contracted-in and arrangements should be considered. The team should also consider any requirement for the development and submission to the customer of a quality plan or an inspection and test plan.

Manufacturing processes
The review team should consider any special processes which may be required and which may have to be supported by special process procedures. The subject of special processes will be dealt with later.

A service organisation should consider:

Customer requirements
Are there any special requirements which are out of the ordinary?

Staffing levels and experience
Consideration should be given to the number of staff required to complete the contract on time, together with the experience and qualifications of such staff.

Organisation
In both a manufacturing and service situation the organisation for contract execution should be determined.

Action by quality assurance
The contract review meeting should be minuted, as in design control.
    The quality assurance representative should then utilise the minutes to verify that any missing or ambiguous information in the contract has been followed up and satisfactorily closed out by the responsible person(s).

General
In the small organisation, both manufacturing and service, where such a formalised review is impracticable, then contract understanding could be

confirmed by utilising a check-list to mark off the requirements. This is a method to confirm that all requirements have been actioned — a type of 'shopping list' so to speak. Very few people have photographic memories, and therefore an *aide-mémoire* should not be thought of as unprofessional. Any form of document, however simple, is worth considering as it can be useful during the latter stages of a contract as objective evidence that an activity was actually carried out.

The author's organisation utilises such check-lists to verify that all the necessary course work, delegate name tags, video equipment, visual aids, and so on, are assembled and correct when presenting a training course.

Documentation preparation, control and retention
This activity is identical to that described for design control.

The documents themselves, however, will be generally of a different nature and will relate to the manufacturing or service requirements and could cover such things as:

    Inspection and test plans
    Testing procedures (mechanical and non-destructive testing)
    Special process procedures (manufacturing and service related)
    Work instruction (manufacturing and service related)
    Mill certification
    Manufacturing processes
    Inspection procedures (manufacturing and service related)

In all cases, the methods of preparing, identifying and approving documents, methods of changing and approving the changes to documents and methods or removing and recalling obsolete documents should be formalised and controlled.

The action by quality assurance would be to verify, initially, the formulation of all necessary procedures to control this activity and to confirm the implementation and adequacy of, and adherence to, the document control system.

Control of inspection, measuring and test equipment
Both manufacturing and service industries utilise equipment which requires some form of regular servicing and/or calibration to confirm its accuracy and its continued fitness for use.

In the first instance, it is necessary to establish the equipment which falls into this category. In general terms, this is equipment which can affect quality.

In a manufacturing environment such equipment would include micrometers, vernier gauges, go and no-go gauges, pressure gauges, mechanical testing machines, jigs, fixtures, templates, and so on.

In a service industry quality can be affected by poor copying machines, word processing equipment, typewriters, and so on.

A system should, therefore, be established which will identify the equipment that is to be calibrated and/or serviced and a calibration and maintenance schedule should be drawn up. This schedule would include such information as:

— Equipment location
— Number or type
— Frequency of calibration or service checks
— Methods of calibration or servicing
— Action that is to be taken in the event of unsatisfactory conditions

Where inspection, measuring and test equipment is to be verified or calibrated against primary master standards, then such master standards should be certified by approved facilities which, in turn, have standards which are verified or calibrated to national standards.

Records should be maintained which detail the frequency and results of calibration and/or servicing and these records should be evaluated on a regular basis to determine the adequacy of the calibration or servicing intervals. It could well be that the calibration intervals of some equipment may have to be reduced due to an increased frequency of use. The reverse may be equally applicable. All such conditions should be documented and the results analysed and actioned.

Where equipment is subject to regular calibration and/or servicing, then the equipment should carry some form of identification label, either adhesive or tie-on. This label should indicate the calibration status, for example the date of last calibration or service plus next calibration date. Where it is not possible to affix a label, due to the configuration or the size of the equipment, then calibration and/or servicing details should be traceable through to the master indexing and scheduling system.

Privately owned equipment, where used to determine finite measurement, should also be included in the calibration system. This is important, as experience has shown that the employees of many manufacturing organisations who purchase and use their own personal measuring equipment quite often feel that, because only they themselves use the equipment and take great care of it, it can never go out of calibration. This is far from the case. In many instances of dimensional error the cause has been traced back to uncalibrated, privately owned equipment. Where such equipment is used as a guide to measurement only and is not used for finite measurement, then it should be marked and carry a statement, such as:

Not to be used for finite measurement—not subject to calibration.

Preferably, however, it should not be used at all.

Equipment which has been checked and found out of calibration, or equipment which has gone over its calibration date and is awaiting calibration, should be labelled to indicate that it is not to be used.

All newly purchased equipment should undergo an initial calibration check to prove its accuracy before being released for use. Again, experience has shown that this is not always the case. Many manufacturing organisations rely on measuring and testing equipment to be accurate just because it is new. How long does it remain new? The author has been shown 'new' equipment which, when traced back to the delivery order, was found to have been in use for well over a year and out of calibration.

Copying machines, computers, and the like, are normally installed by the manufacturers or their agents and undergo a calibration or fitness for use check before handing over to the customer. This can be regarded as a calibration check prior to use but the owner should be satisfied before acceptance.

Many large organisations have a great deal of equipment to calibrate or service. Such cases could utilise a computer program to update and control this activity.

The smaller organisation would normally utilise a card indexing system or a record book. Whatever the system used it should be the responsibility of one person or department.

It is recommended that the production department should take the responsibility as it is this department that is responsible for the quality of the hardware it produces. It should not rely on others, such as a quality control department, to do this work for them.

The action by quality assurance would be initially to verify the establishment of the calibration and/or servicing system and to monitor its implementation, effectiveness and adherence.

Control of purchased materiel and services

This activity is applicable to all industries and levels of quality programme.

The customer should verify the adequacy of his prime purchasing sources. Similarly the contractor will verify the adequacy of subcontracted sources and so on down the line. The customer should not have to evaluate the adequacy of any supply source other than the first party source.

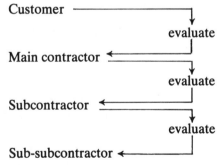

Unfortunately this is far from general practice, as many customers are still experiencing a great reluctance on the part of their main contractors to evaluate subcontracting sources. This surely must place an unnecessary burden on the customer's time and resources and take the responsibility away from the organisation to whom it should belong. Augustus de Morgan (1806–1871) has been quoted as saying: 'Great fleas have little fleas upon their backs to bite 'em, and little fleas have lesser fleas and so ad infinitum.' This is how it should be in the case of customer, contractor and subcontractor procurement sources.

The methods of controlling purchased materiel and services have already been dealt with in detail in Chapter 12.

Incoming inspection

This activity is carried out to verify the acceptability and condition of bought-out materiel. It is one method of assessing a supplier's capability but it is a method not to be relied upon where tight schedules are concerned. An incoming inspection will serve only to verify whether an item is acceptable or not. If it is not acceptable then, of course, a decision has to be made whether to scrap and reorder, return to the supplier for rework or repair in-house. Whichever decision is made, there will inevitably be a delay in attaining fitness for use.

Other methods of assessing capability have already been discussed.

The methods to be used during an incoming inspection activity will depend upon the nature and quantity of the materiel. Such information should be incorporated into an inspection and test plan and would include:

> Inspection and test requirements
> Sampling methods (if required)
> Documentation requirements
> Acceptance/rejection criteria

as has been described previously in Chapter 10.

Any item which is received without the required supporting documentation should preferably be withheld from production pending the receipt and acceptance of such documentation, or if such items are released for production, then there should be a means of recalling the items if problems subsequently arise.

Items rejected upon receipt should be identified as rejected and placed in a quarantined area pending a decision on the action to be taken.

Incoming inspection is normally carried out by a company's quality control or inspection department, although other qualified personnel could do it provided such responsibility is clearly defined. The results of all such inspections should be documented. Inspection results can be utilised to evaluate supplier performance and, as for any type of information, the results should be made available to the people who need to know. There is no point in the quality control or inspection department keeping detailed analyses of incoming inspection results if these are not made known to the engineering or purchasing departments.

Engineering should be aware of problems as they may reflect upon a specification. For example, it may be found that the specification is too tight and requires amendment.

Purchasing should be aware of supplier performance in order to update their records.

Again—communication is important.

In the case of service organisations most, if not all, bought-out items should be checked upon receipt. Normally the person responsible for the purchase would carry out this activity. Office or service routines (work instructions) should indicate responsibilities and action to be taken in the event of unacceptable items.

The action by quality assurance would be to verify the establishment of the appropriate inspection and test plans, procedures or routines and confirm implementation, effectiveness and adherence.

Purchaser-supplied materiel

This could be termed 'free issue materiel'. It is materiel supplied free of charge by a customer for use on a given contract. Materiel may be supplied free of charge to both manufacturing and service organisations.

Although the majority of quality assurance standards include the control of purchaser (customer) supplied materiel in the list of criteria, it is necessary only to implement such a system if an organisation is regularly in receipt of such materiel. Do not implement a system for control just because it is listed in a quality assurance standard! Unfortunately many organisations, and many quality assurance consultants for that matter, are of the opinion that to comply with a given quality assurance standard one must implement every control listed in that standard. This is certainly not the case and this is one control that falls into that category.

To explain more fully the exact nature of purchaser-supplied materiel, it is worthwhile looking at some examples.

In a service industry there may be many areas of free issue materiel:

— A house decorator may be supplied by the customer with paint and paper which he is to apply.
— A printer may be supplied by the customer with special paper.
— A public service worker may be supplied with a free uniform.

   and so on.

In a manufacturing industry it is not uncommon, especially in offshore oil and gas, for the customer to purchase the material for a jacket structure and supply it, free of charge, to a fabrication yard where it will be 'made up' into the jacket.

Whenever materiel is supplied 'free issue', it should be under strict control from initial receipt until despatch as, or part of, a finished product. Or, in the case of free issue clothing, from receipt until the end of its requirement or useful life. A system for this control should be documented.

Initially, all materiel supplied by the customer should be inspected on receipt for damage, completeness and for compliance with contract requirements. Any special storage and handling instructions should be complied with.

During storage inspection should be carried out on a regular basis, either by the production department or by a quality control inspector, to verify condition. Adequacy of the storage facilities should be reviewed at the same time and shelf life conditions may also be evaluated where necessary.

If, during storage, any damage or unsatisfactory conditions are observed then, of course, the customer should be advised and action taken to determine the cause and prevent a recurrence of the condition.

The system should also ensure that all documentation received with the materiel is correct and that any deficiencies, or abnormalities, are reported to the customer for verification and action.

All deficient or defective customer-supplied materiel should be marked, segregated and placed in a quarantined area where it will be protected and prohibited from use.

Any testing which may be required by the customer should be conducted on receipt and prior to use, and the results documented.

A separate storage area should be set aside for customer-supplied materiel and the necessary records should be maintained to identify to the customer where and when such materiel was used.

In the case of a steel jacket fabrication for example, there will, in all probability, be a requirement for the fabricator to control and store, for the customer's eventual disposal, all the steel off-cuts. The customer will have supplied a known quantity of steel. A given number of tonnes will be used in building the jacket and the remainder, either in whole plate or off-cuts, will need to be accounted for to the customer for disposal. Hence the requirement for the maintenance of records.

The development of a system to control purchaser (customer) supplied materiel can be developed only with customer participation. Any non-conforming materiel cannot be handled in the same way as one's own non-conforming materiel. The customer must always be involved, as it is the customer who will determine the action to be taken for its disposition.

The action by quality assurance should be to determine that customer requirements relating to the control of free issue materiel have been incorporated into an appropriate procedure and then to verify, by audit, that such requirements are being implemented and that the system is effective and being adhered to.

In-process inspection

All requirements for in-process inspection should be included in the inspection and test plan. The requirements would include the points during manufacture where inspection is required and whether manufacture should cease until the inspection has been carried out (mandatory hold point). The type of inspection (visual, dimensional or non-destructive test) should be indicated and also whether any sampling schemes are to be used.

As each inspection and/or test is completed, it should be recorded on an appropriate document, usually the relevant manufacturing route card (Fig. 13.2 is a typical routing card for machine-shop activities).

Non-conforming items should be dealt with in accordance with a written procedure established for such an activity.

Initially, the machine operator should be responsible for checking his own work (the self-check). Wherever possible this should be the only check necessary. By making the operator responsible for his own quality, there should be a reduction in the inspection work-force leading to a reduction in subsequent rectification work.

	JOB No.	DRAWING	PATTERN	PAGE	ITEM	MAT	QUANTITY

DESCRIPTION:	DO NOT WORK TO THIS SKETCH:
DATE:	

ROUTED BY:	DATE REQUIRED:	INSPECTED BY:

OPERATION:		SET UP	EACH
		ADD FOR FIRST PIECES %	
	MACH No.	ADD FOR NEXT PIECES %	

OPERATION:		SET UP	EACH
		ADD FOR FIRST PIECES %	
	MACH No.	ADD FOR NEXT PIECES %	

OPERATION:		SET UP	EACH
		ADD FOR FIRST PIECES %	
	MACH No.	ADD FOR NEXT PIECES %	

OPERATION:		SET UP	EACH
		ADD FOR FIRST PIECES %	
	MACH No.	ADD FOR NEXT PIECES %	

OPERATION:		SET UP	EACH
		ADD FOR FIRST PIECES %	
	MACH No.	ADD FOR NEXT PIECES %	

OPERATION:		SET UP	EACH
		ADD FOR FIRST PIECES %	
	MACH No.	ADD FOR NEXT PIECES %	

AFTER INSPECTION DELIVER TO:
MAT'L. REQ'D.

XYZ-MNF-009.3

Fig. 13.2 — Route card.

Conversations with management and engineering personnel often suggest that a requirement for increased 'QA/QC' to overcome quality problems in manufacturing is necessary, whereas what is really required is an increase in 'QA' (prevention) with a decrease in 'QC' (cure).

Whoever is responsible for in-process inspection should document the results and all data maintained for subsequent evaluation.

Service organisations carry out a form of in-process inspection, although in many instances it is not recognised as such. Normally supervisory staff evaluate work as it progresses.

The responsibility of quality assurance would be to verify, as for all other activities, the establishment, implementation, and effectiveness of and the adherence to the documented system for in-process inspection.

Final inspection

As for in-process inspection, all requirements for final inspection should be included in the inspection and test plan. The requirements would include the type and nature of the inspection to be carried out, together with any testing which is to be undertaken and which the customer and/or regulatory body may wish to witness. In the case of large batches of identical items, sampling methods should also be indicated.

The inspection and test plan should also include documentation which will be required to verify the acceptibility of the item, such as:

>   Material certificates
>   Functional test results
>   Non-destructive test results
>   Sampling results
>   Dimensional results
>   and so on

In the case of non-compliant items, then such should be identified and quarantined pending arrangements for dispositioning, which would be carried out in accordance with a procedure for non-conforming items.

The acceptability of an item should be indicated on the appropriate documentation.

The procedure adopted for in-house final inspection would apply also to purchased items where final inspection is to be carried out by the purchaser at a subcontractor's premises.

Service organisations also carry out forms of final inspection.

For example, the work of hotel room cleaning staff is generally checked by a supervisor against a check-list to verify that not only is the room clean but to confirm that clean towels, soap, shoe-cleaning cloths, tea-making facilities, and so on, have been taken care of.

The responsibility of quality assurance would be to verify, as for all other activities, the establishment and effectiveness of, and the adherence to, the documented system for final inspection.

Sampling (where applicable)

As for purchaser-supplied (free issue) materiel, the majority of quality assurance standards include sampling schemes as one of the criteria. There are many organisations who do not manufacture identical items in sufficient quantities to warrant the use of sampling schemes and, in such cases, it would not be necessary to establish a system for such.

Where considerable numbers of identical items are produced, then it is beneficial to introduce a sampling scheme which will, in all probability, be based upon an applicable standard.

Sampling schemes are established to give the manufacturer and the purchaser the confidence that an acceptable quality level (not to be confused with programme level) has been achieved.

It has been proved that a well-designed sampling scheme can achieve the same level of confidence as a 100% inspection.

Experience has shown that given 100 items to inspect for dimension and finish there will be as many different acceptance levels as there are inspectors taking part. Or, to make the point another way, give a number of people the same page from a book and ask them to count the number of R's on the page, then the probability is that there will be as many different answers as there are people taking part in the exercise.

In such cases where sampling schemes are utilised, such schemes should be indicated on the inspection and test plan.

So much has been written on sampling techniques that the author has no intention of adding to the myriad of publications on the subject. Suffice to say that a number of standards and publications dealing with sampling and statistical quality control are included in the bibliography.

Service organisations can also utilise sampling schemes where considerable numbers of identical functions are carried out. One area which lends itself to sampling is the reproduction of identical documents which are to be distributed to many individuals—the 'mail shot'. Word processors are utilised to make this operation much more effective but even then there is no guarantee of 100% correctness.

The action by quality assurance should be to verify that the requirements for sampling have been established and that such are being effectively implemented.

Inspection status

There should be some means of identifying the status of an item during production. By this is meant an identification system which would indicate at a glance whether an item (or items) is (or are) awaiting inspection, has (or have) been inspected and accepted or inspected and rejected.

Inspection status is invariably overlooked by many organisations and a lack of an identification system has caused many problems due to rejected items being processed further only to be re-rejected later on.

Many times during the auditing of manufacturing organisations it has been found necessary to request the status of manufactured items because no positive identification methods were used. The time involved in obtaining the answers to such requests was quite considerable.

On one such occasion it meant tracing the whereabouts of the chief inspector, as he was the only person who had the information. The manufacturing facility concerned covered a wide area and the chief inspector could have been in any one of a dozen places. By the time a positive indication of his location was found, he had gone to lunch! In all, it took three hours to obtain the required information. This is far from an isolated incident.

A simple identification system, known to all shop-floor personnel, would have saved the time of all the people involved, not to mention the frustration experienced by all concerned.

Some form of positive identification of status should be used. The methods are, as for most other systems, a matter of company choice. For example, a typical system would be:

> Items or batches awaiting inspection are unmarked.
> Items or batches inspected and accepted are tagged with green adhesive labels.
> Items or batches inspected and rejected are tagged with red adhesive labels or 'rejected' tags.

Whatever system is used, it should be documented and implemented without variation.

The authority for the application or removal of any identification labels or stickers should be documented; such authority is usually given to the quality control department.

Service organisations can utilise an inspection status system to identify the acceptability, or otherwise, of a process or function during an activity.

The action by quality assurance would be to verify the establishment of a suitable identification system and confirm its implementation and effectiveness.

Identification and traceability

Traceability is generally a requirement only by contract and is, therefore, another of the criteria of the quality assurance standards which is not applicable to all organisations. It would not normally apply to any service-related organisation.

The subject of traceability was introduced in design control, when it was established that it should be the responsibility of the relevant design engineer to determine which items require traceability.

Having established the requirement in the design stage, this requirement would be written into the specification.

The manufacturing organisation should then inject such traceability requirements into its own production planning system and inspection and test plan.

A method of identifying the items or batches which require traceability should be established. This identification method should be unique to the contract and will be carried through all stages of manufacture and on to installation and thence throughout the operational life of the unit.

This unique identification should be recorded on all applicable documentation.

The action by quality assurance would be to verify the requirement for identification and traceability, and to audit the implementation of the system.

Handling and storage

All items received into either a manufacturing or service organisation should be stored and protected against misuse, damage and deterioration, and also controlled against unauthorised use.

Once cleared through incoming inspection, items generally go into store pending use.

Similarly, items which are being processed through a manufacturing cycle can go into store pending further processing. For example, material which has to undergo planing and drilling could complete the planing process and then go into store pending the drilling operation. In such cases, there would be a requirement for protection of the surface finish against corrosion and damage.

Storage should be controlled so that any items subject to deterioration due to limited 'shelf life' are released in strict rotation.

Items subject to corrosion should be stored in the appropriate environmental conditions where humidity and temperature can be regulated to minimise corrosion.

It is strongly recommended that entry to all storage areas should be limited to authorised personnel only, so as to prevent unauthorised use of materiel.

Experience has shown that such limited access to storage areas is not generally practised and shop-floor personnel are able to obtain materiel from stores without control. Apart from the security aspect (which is probably such that materiel could not leave the premises), such a free-for-all attitude does nothing to eliminate damage, use of expired shelf life components, and the like, not to mention disturbance of records.

Not only should storage areas be of limited access but regular monitoring of the storage of items during processing should be carried out.

Any unsatisfactory conditions brought to light during monitoring should be dealt with in accordance with an appropriate system.

The normal practice is for the monitoring of storage facilities to be carried out by quality control personnel, but this is surely a function which should be undertaken by responsible production personnel. Production should be made responsible for the quality of the work they produce and not rely on others to do it for them.

The action by quality assurance would be to verify the establishment of the appropriate handling and storage system, and to audit implementation.

Special processes

Special processes are processes which cannot be verified as having been properly carried out by final inspection or testing. In other words, processes which require continuous or intermittent monitoring throughout.

Special processes fall into two distinct categories: those relating to manufacture and those relating to inspection and testing.

The manufacturing special processes include such things as:

Welding
Casting
Concrete mixing
Protective coatings
Heat treatment

The inspection and testing special processes include such things as:

Radiography
Magnetic particle inspection
Dye penetrant inspection
Ultrasonic inspection
Pressure testing

It should be noted that some everyday activities are listed among these special processes: welding, heat treatment and non-destructive testing. Problems arise because such activities are not regarded as 'special'! If they are treated as special, and the necessary control procedures developed and implemented, then many of these problems can be prevented. To quote some examples:

In the case of protective coating (painting), all that one is able to establish at final inspection is that the coating thickness and colour are correct. Final inspection will not confirm that the surface finish of the base material was in accordance with specification, neither will it confirm the thickness of the ground coat, undercoats and finish coat. It will also not confirm whether the curing (time, temperature and humidity) process was carried out to specification.

In the case of welding, it is not possible to verify at final inspection whether the consumables were temperature and time controlled, whether the correct pre-heat temperature was attained, and so on.

All that a heat treatment graph will convey is that the temperature rise, hold and reduce were carried out according to specification. What the graph will not disclose is whether other items were placed in the oven at the same time, whether the item itself was placed in the correct location in the oven and whether the thermocouples were correctly situated.

The quality of a special process cannot usually be verified by subsequent inspection and testing of the processed material. It will, therefore, be necessary to establish full conformance by evidence obtained during the process. This is achievable by:

(1) Establishing documented procedures which will ensure that all special processes are carried out under controlled conditions by qualified personnel using calibrated equipment in accordance with applicable contract codes, specifications, standards and regulatory requirements.
(2) Maintaining current records of qualified personnel, equipment and processes, in accordance with the requirements of the applicable codes and standards.
(3) Defining the necessary qualifications of personnel, equipment and processes not covered by existing codes or standards, or when contractual clauses define stricter requirements than those already established.

Service organisations also have a requirement to establish special process procedures and there are some manufacturing processes which are equally applicable to service organisations. These processes include:

X-ray
Ultrasonics
Heat treatment

which are used mainly in hospital services.

The action by quality assurance would be to verify that the processes which are classified as special are procedurally controlled. Such controls would include: maintenance and calibration of special process equipment and the suitability of personnel performing special processes; to audit the implementation and effectiveness of, and adherence to, the system and to verify the utilisation of qualified personnel.

Preservation, packaging and shipping

Where preservation, packaging and shipping requirements are not defined by contract, then a system should be developed to assure the effectiveness of this function.

The system should define the methods of preserving and packaging items to assure cleanliness, prevention of damage and preservation during shipment and possible storage at final destination. Such details should be included in the inspection and test plan.

Prior to shipment the acceptability of the item should be verified. Verification should include the adequacy of preservation and packaging, together with the inclusion of correct documentation.

The methods of transportation, where not defined in the contract, should be such to ensure safe arrival at destination.

Inadequate packing and inappropriate transport facilities are the causes of much customer dissatisfaction. Regardless of the care taken to assure the quality of an item, all this can be negated by the item being lost in transit, arriving late or arriving in a damaged condition.

Fitness for purpose is the condition received for use.

Service organisations also have a responsibility to respond to requirements for preservation, packaging and shipping.

For example, documents (legal, banking and so on) should be packed and shipped (posted) to be received by customer on time and in a fit for purpose condition.

The action by quality assurance should be to verify the inclusion of preservation, packaging and shipping details in the inspection and test plan, and to audit the implementation and effectiveness of the system.

Non-conforming items

Any inspection process can result in an item being found unsuitable. This can occur upon receipt, during manufacture or at final inspection. Whenever it does occur, there should be a system to direct personnel in the actions to be taken.

Initially, a non-conforming item should be identified as being non-conforming with a suitable tag, adhesive label or paint mark. It should then, wherever possible, be segregated from all other items to prevent unauthorised use, shipment or inclusion with conforming items.

The applicable documentation should then be completed, which should identify the item, the nature of the defect or discrepancy. The documentation should then be forwarded to the appropriate department for review.

It will be the responsibility of the appropriate person to determine the action to be taken. In some instances, particularly in cases of high-value or safety-related equipment, it could be necessary to set up a review board to discuss the implications of the discrepancy. In any event, the outcome will be one of the following:

Scrap
Repair or rework
Use as is

The level of authority at which dispositioning of non-conforming items can be made should be clearly established. For example, deviations of a minor nature could well be handled by inspection personnel, provided the necessary rework or repair procedures have been agreed previously.

All other deviations should be dealt with by reference back to the original design source, which may well include customer participation. Whatever the outcome, the system should ensure that the appropriate action is taken and documented.

Service organisations will also have a requirement to comply where a service has been unacceptable to the customer.

The action by quality assurance should be to verify that the system for dealing with non-conforming items is established and to monitor, as required, its implementation and effectiveness.

Records

All quality assurance standards call for a system to control records, which could be defined in three words: filing and finding.

The filing of the records and the ability to find such records with the minimum of time and effort is the hallmark of a well-organised document control system.

In the main the records, which are to be developed and maintained, relate to what are described as quality-related activities. These records provide the objective evidence that an item, or service, meets contract or specification requirements, and it is this objective evidence which the quality assurance auditor will seek to confirm compliance with the system. (Auditing is dealt with in Chapter 15).

Records would comprise such items as:

(1) System and compliance audit reports.
(2) Results of inspections performed in accordance with the inspection and test plan.
(3) Data covering the reliability of purchasing sources.
(4) Material certification.
(5) Data covering the calibration of inspection, measuring and test equipment.
(6) Details of non-conforming items.
(7) Details of corrective actions.
(8) Results of inspection of stores areas.
(9) Results of tests, approvals and audits by customers, regulatory bodies and other third party sources.
(10) Certification for approval of personnel.
(11) Functional test reports and data.
(12) Installation and commissioning test reports.

All records should be reviewed and evaluated regularly by responsible personnel. The results of such reviews should be used for the purpose of improving and updating the quality systems.

Records should be retained for the period set by legislation or by the contract (whichever is the maximum).

Records should be stored in a suitable environment which will minimise deterioration or damage, and prevent loss. In normal circumstances, this should be in steel cabinets which are water-resistant and fire-retardant.

Other methods of record retention may be used, such as computerised data storage, microfilm or microfiche, but such should be agreed with the customer where necessary.

Service organisations will also have a requirement to maintain and retain records.

The action by quality assurance should be to verify the establishment of the record system and to monitor, by audit, the implementation and effectiveness of, and the adherence to, the system.

Training

Not all quality assurance standards identify the requirement for training of personnel, yet it is a most important activity.

Training can be required in many areas in both manufacturing and service environments. The introduction of new machinery and equipment, the upgrading of personnel to meet new employment criteria, the retraining of operatives to take on additional responsibilities and to meet the demands of new technology, are just some of the areas which should be covered by a corporate training policy.

In determining training requirements, consideration should be given to those functions which require acquired skills and those functions which could be adversely affected by lack of skill. Such functions should be identified, categorised and documented.

The following is a non-exhaustive list of functions which could be considered as requiring skills which should be covered by training:

Manufacturing	*Services*
Quality assurance management	Quality assurance management
Auditing (internal and external)	Auditing (internal)
Welding	Word processing
Ultrasonic examination	Telephone answering
Magnetic particle examination	Computing
Radiography	Radiography
Penetrant examination	

Management should establish, by review, examination, or other means, whether personnel carrying out such functions require training or additional experience to make good any shortfall. Management should also establish how competence in a given function is determined, by examination, testing, certification, and so on.

The methods to be used in making good such shortfall in experience or training should also be documented and would include training or indoctrination by in-house training schemes or by third party training organisations.

Records of training involvement, together with examination or test results (where applicable), should be documented and made available to the customer or regulatory body as required.

Training in certain functions requires regular updating and the necessary evidence that such retraining or maintenance of qualifications has been carried out should be documented. For example, welders and weld inspectors require retesting at regular intervals to retain qualification; quality assurance lead assessors require re-evaluation on a regular basis to retain registration, and so on.

The action by quality assurance should be: to verify the establishment of a training policy and to monitor, by audit, that the requirements of such a policy are being implemented; to verify that personnel are receiving, or have received, the training as required and that qualification and requalification records are maintained and updated.

Audit and corrective action

The quality assurance department would verify, initially, the establishment of procedures to control all the foregoing activities and then to monitor, by audit, their implementation, adherence and effectiveness.

All non-conformances exposed during audits would be addressed by corrective action requests upon the appropriate party, with follow-up action to verify that corrective action had been taken and steps taken to prevent a recurrence of the deficiency.

Once manufacture is complete, the item is either delivered to the customer for use or it is to be installed and commissioned. The next act in the total presentation is installation control.

14

Installation control

The control of installation processes is a very neglected area. There are a number of quality assurance standards that refer to installation in the title yet very little guidance is given on the subject in the standard itself.

In the main, the control of installation covers the same criteria as manufacture and it is to manufacturing control that one should look to determine the procedural requirements.

THE MAJOR ACTIVITIES

Again, as for previous elements, or acts, in the total presentation, the most important activities have been tabulated (Fig. 14.1). As previously, each activity is dealt with in detail.

Contract review (planning)

Should a contract cover installation activities only then, of course, should a complete formal contract review meeting take place to review the customer requirements and to plan for the installation. If, however, as is most likely to be the case, installation forms only part of a total package, then the contract review meeting should have taken place previously. Nevertheless, before the installation activity, a review of requirements should take place and all functions planned in a systematic manner.

All concerned should be aware of their responsibilities and, if necessary, a review team assembled to review the requirements and plan for the installation of the equipment or plant.

Installation requirements

The planning for installation will entail a detailed consideration of the installation requirements and a verification that the requirements are fully understood by all involved personnel.

Specifications and standards

It should be confirmed that all applicable specifications and standards are available to the installation team and of the correct issue. If there should be

INSTALLATION CONTROL

ACTIVITY	SCOPE	PERFORMED BY	ACTION BY QA
1 Contract review (planning)	Review: Installation requirements Specifications and standards Materials Tools Installation processes Inspection, test and commissioning requirements Organisation	Site management Installation Quality control (site) Quality assurance	Verify that missing or ambiguous information has been followed up and satisfactorily closed out by the responsible person
2 Document preparation control and retention	Ensure correct and uniform presentation of documents. Ensure formal preparation identification, checking, approval and distribution, including amendments. Verify retention, retrieval, storage and handover requirements	Site management Installation Quality control (site)	Audit adherence to procedure
3 Control of inspection Measuring and test equipment	Verify: Equipment to be controlled Standards for control Calibration method Calibration interval Identification of calibration status	Site management Production	Audit adherence to procedure
4 Control of locally purchased materiel and services	Assure methods of adequately assessing supplier's ability to meet contract requirements	Site purchasing Installation Quality control (site)	Audit adherence to procedure
5 Incoming inspection at site	Verify materiel conformity to requirements	Quality control (site)	Audit adherence to inspection, test and commissioning plan
6 Purchaser-supplied materiel (manufacturer-supplied)	Verify: Unpacking methods Type, condition and quantity on receipt Storage requirements	Quality control (site)	Audit adherence to inspection, test and commissioning plan
7 Inspection during installation (in-process inspection)	Verify adherence to specification during installation by inspection and/or test. Identification. Documentation	Quality control (site)	Audit adherence to inspection, test and commissioning plan
8 Final inspection	Verify adherence to specification on completion by inspection and/or test. Identification. Documentation	Quality control (site)	Audit adherence to inspection, test and commissioning plan
9 Sampling (where applicable)	Verify use of sampling schemes Methods Standards	Quality control (site)	Audit adherence to inspection, test and commissioning plan
10 Inspection, commissioning status	Verify methods of indicating inspection and/or commissioning status	Commissioning personnel Quality control (site)	Audit adherence to procedure
11 Identification and traceability (where applicable)	Verify requirements for traceability of materiel. Identification. Documentation	Installation Quality control (site)	Audit adherence to inspection, test and commissioning plan
12 Handling and storage	Verify handling and storage methods	Installation Quality control (site)	Audit adherence to inspection, test and commissioning plan
13 Special processes	Verify which installation processes fall into the special category. Determine methods of control, maintenance and calibration of special process equipment. Suitability of personnel performing special processes	Installation Quality control (site)	Audit adherence to procedure
14 Non-conforming items or processes	Verify methods of identifying and dispositioning non-conforming items or processes	Installation Commissioning Quality control (site)	Audit adherence to procedure
15 Records	Verify: Requirements Format Contents Storage Retrieval Retention period	Library Site document control centre	Audit adherence to procedure
16 Training	Verify and document training needs Methods Records	Management Installation	Audit adherence to procedure
17 Audit and corrective action	Ensure non-conformances promptly identified and corrective action taken to prevent recurrence	Site management Installation Quality assurance	Audit adherence to procedure

Fig. 14.1 — Installation matrix.

any shortfalls or ambiguities, these should be resolved before the installation activity commences.

Materials
It should be ensured that the correct materials and equipment are available and that such are properly identified. In the case of unassembled units, each section of the unit should be match-marked to facilitate installation. This latter requirement is most important, as experience has shown that a great deal of time can be expended by installation teams trying to verify which piece goes where. Mistakes can also be made by installing almost identical parts in the wrong location, only to discover the error much later on and thus have to redo all the work to rectify the fault.

Tools
The need for special installation tools should also be considered. It may be necessary to purchase or hire specialised equipment.

Installation processes
Consideration should be given to the use of any special installation processes, which may have to be supported by special process procedures.

Inspection, test and commissioning requirements
An inspection, test and commissioning plan should be developed which should take into consideration any special requirements imposed by contract. Specialised testing and/or commissioning equipment may have to be contracted-in and arrangements for either purchase or hire should be considered.

Organisation
The organisation structure of the installation and commissioning team should be established, together with any customer interfaces. Consideration should also be given to the staffing requirements, together with experience and qualification levels.

General
In the case of consumer products such as washing machines, central heating units, double glazing and so on, the planning for installation and commissioning would take place but on a much smaller scale. In many instances, installation is a one-person operation but, nevertheless, that person should make sure before undertaking an installation process that all the materials, equipment, tools, testing procedures and the like are available, in order that the installation and commissioning activities are carried out correctly and efficiently.

Action by quality assurance
In the case of an installation only contract, the contract review meeting should be minuted. The quality assurance representative should verify that

any missing or ambiguous information in the contract has been followed up and closed out by the responsible person(s).

In the case where the installation process is part of a total package, then in all probability the planning activity for installation would be established in the form of an installation and commissioning plan, which the quality assurance representative would verify as having been established.

Document preparation, control and retention

This activity is identical to that described for design control but the documents themselves will be generally of a different nature and will relate to the installation and commissioning requirements and could cover such things as:

> Installation procedures
> Inspection, test and commissioning plans
> Testing and commissioning procedures
> Special process procedures for installation and commissioning
> Work instructions
> Inspection procedures

In all cases, the methods of preparing, identifying and approving documents, methods of changing and approving changes to documents and methods of removing and recalling obsolete documents should be formalised and controlled.

The action by quality assurance should be to verify, initially, the formulation of all relevant procedures to control this activity and to confirm the implementation and adequacy of, and adherence to, the document control system.

Control of inspection, measuring and test equipment

The installation and commissioning activities will, in all probability, utilise equipment which requires some form of regular servicing and/or calibration to confirm its accuracy and its continued fitness for use.

The methods for such control are identical to those detailed in Chapter 13 but, depending on the size and nature of the equipment or plant to be installed, the calibration centre could well be located at the installation site with its own master standards and its own gauge room.

A petrochemical or power production plant are cases in point. The actual installation process is at the site itself and, when commissioned, the plant will continue to be operated and maintained for many years, thus inspection and test equipment will be in regular use at the site location.

With small items of equipment, however, where installation and commissioning are part of a total contract, then of course measuring, test and inspection equipment would be drawn from stores by the installation crew (which may comprise one or more personnel). The stores would be located in the manufacturing facility and, therefore, the calibration of such equipment would be controlled, for example, by the production department.

The action by quality assurance should be to verify the calibration status of equipment used by installation personnel.

Control of locally purchased materiel and services
In the main, personnel will be installing materiel supplied by others (i.e. their own manufactured items or items supplied by the customer) and there should be no requirement to purchase additional materiel or services.

In the case of large projects such as petrochemical or power production plants mentioned earlier there will, in all probability, be a project management team established on-site. A good deal of materiel and services will have to be purchased locally and could comprise:

Materiel	*Services*
Consumables	Welders
Structural steel	Inspection and
Plate material	non-destructive testing
Fasteners	personnel

In this case site management should evaluate procurement sources in the same manner as for procurement control (Chapter 12).

The action by quality assurance will be exactly as before.

Incoming inspection at site
As for manufacturing control, this activity is carried out to verify the acceptability and condition of bought-out materiel.

This activity should be formalised both in the case of the large projects already mentioned, and also in very small installation tasks where it may be done without the installer actually recognising the fact. As an example, a technician who installs a washing machine may require a pipe fitting not supplied with the machine. The installer goes through two functions:

(1) He identifies the procurement source (possibly a local hardware store).
(2) He inspects the item for conformance.

If he actually goes to the store himself, inspection will be carried out at source. If the item is sent by the store or is collected by the installer's helper, then inspection is carried out on arrival (incoming inspection at site).

In all probability, the method for dealing with this case will have been established by the washing machine manufacturer and should be recognised as being the most effective method of dealing with such a circumstance. Is it, however, as effective or efficient as one might suppose? How much simpler to have included in the installation kit a set of pipe fittings to cover all possibilities! The cost of the time taken in first identifying the procurement source and then collecting the part (at most wholesale outlets there is usually a long wait to be served) will be, in all probability, far in excess of the cost of the part!

Many organisations fail to realise the time involved in rectifying a problem. In times of high labour costs this can be very significant.

The action by quality assurance is twofold. In the case of the large project situation it should be to verify, as in manufacturing control, the establishment of the appropriate inspection and test plan which will call up incoming inspection as required.

In the case of our washing machine installer, quality assurance should be aware of such circumstances and should draw management's attention to the inefficiency of such practices. It will mean, of course, that the installer should have the means of communicating back to base and that such communications are distributed on the 'need to know' basis and not kept just for reference in the shipping or such other department. Management can act only if it is aware of the problem.

It should not be assumed that only washing machine manufacturers adopt such procedures. Most organisations who supply and install their own products do leave their installers to purchase locally whatever has been forgotten. The author has experienced similar situations with respect to double glazing, central heating, home extensions, and others. There is nothing worse than looking at a gaping hole where a window should be because some part or other was not included in the shipment and the local supply source was temporarily out of stock of that part.

Purchaser-supplied materiel (manufacturer-supplied)

This activity could be said to be more applicable to the construction and installation site than to the manufacturing process. Most materiel to be installed will have been supplied to the installer by someone else. In the case of our washing machine installer, the machine would have been supplied to him by the company who employs him. In the case of the large construction and installation site, the materiel would have been supplied by the central purchasing body.

In either case, it should be regarded as 'free issue' and the necessary controls implemented to verify its completeness and freedom from damage.

British Standard 5750 gives the following definition:

> Purchaser supplied materiel is materiel owned by the purchaser and furnished to the supplier for his use in meeting the requirements of the contract. Where the supplier takes delivery, he has to realise that he is accepting full responsibility for freedom from damage, identification, maintenance, storage, handling and use while the materiel is in his possession.

The installer or, in the case of large projects, site management, should therefore ensure that there are satisfactory arrangements for the following:

> Examination of the materiel upon receipt to check quantities, identities, and to detect any damage caused during transit.
>
> Periodic inspection during storage to detect any sign of deterioration, to check on any outdating risk where storage time exceeds recommended shelf life; to ensure the maintenance of storage conditions which will not cause deterioration and to check generally the

condition of stored materiel.

Compliance with any contractual requirement for reinspection, appropriate identification and safeguarding of materiel to prevent unauthorised use or improper disposal.

Procedures should exist which define the manner in which any shortages, damage or other factors rendering the materiel unfit for use are reported to the customer.

The action by quality assurance should be to determine that the installer or site management are aware of, and have access to, procedures as described above and to verify their implementation and effectiveness.

Inspection during installation (in-process inspection)
The requirements for inspection during installation should be documented. The inspection and test plan described in Chapter 10 would be the ideal vehicle for this activity.

The requirements would include the points during installation where the installer (or installation crew) would cease pending an intermediate check to verify acceptance at a given point. The type of acceptance check or test should be indicated.

As each acceptance check or test is completed, it should be reported on an appropriate document—the installation check-list, for example, could include the facility for this.

As for any activity, the installation personnel should be responsible for checking their own work before calling on the appropriate inspection personnel to verify acceptability. In the case of the domestic appliance installer, he will, in all probability, be working alone and will undertake the verification activity himself. The use of a check-list in such situations is, therefore, most important.

The action by quality assurance would be to verify, as for all other activities, the establishment, implementation and effectiveness of, and the adherence to, the documented system for inspection during installation.

Final inspection
As for inspection during installation, all requirements for final inspection on completion of the installation process should be included in the appropriate document, such as the inspection and test plan.

As for manufacturing control, the requirement would include the type and nature of the inspection to be carried out, together with any testing which is to be undertaken and which the customer and/or regulatory body may wish to witness.

The requirements for regulatory body involvement are not unique to large projects in this respect. The installation of domestic gas and electrical appliances has in some instances, in many countries, to be checked for safety aspects by an accredited agency prior to 'switch-on' and release, for use, to the customer.

All such requirements should be established before installation and taken into consideration. This serves, once again, to confirm the importance of the planning or contract review activity, which should be carried out regardless of the quality programme level or the size and nature of the contract.

The action by quality assurance would be to verify that the necessary planning had been carried out and that final inspection requirements are understood and are effectively implemented.

Sampling
In all probability sampling would not be applicable during installation but should it be so then such requirements would be dealt with in the same manner as for manufacturing control.

Inspection and commissioning status
As for manufacturing, there should be some means of identifying the status of an item or system (mechanical, electrical, instrumentation, and so on) during installation and eventual commissioning.

Again, as for manufacturing, the identification system should indicate, at a glance, and at any point during the installation and commissioning process, whether an item or system is awaiting inspection (or commissioning), has been inspected and accepted (commissioned) or inspected and rejected (failed commissioning test).

The methods and procedures for such identification are, as for most other systems, a matter of company choice and the example given for manufacturing control could be adapted to suit the installation and commissioning process.

The action by quality assurance would be to verify the establishment of a suitable identification system and confirm its implementation and effectiveness.

Identification and traceability
As has already been said, traceability is generally a requirement only by contract and, in such instances, should operate throughout the design, manufacture, installation and operational life of the unit.

Traceability requirements were established and discussed during design control, carried through manufacturing control and should now be implemented during installation.

The traceability requirements should be detailed in the installation planning system and the inspection, test and commissioning plan.

The items requiring traceability should have already been identified during manufacture. During installation, the location of such items in the plant layout should be documented, together with the unique identification number, or symbol, of the unit. This information should, of course, be relayed back to 'central records' to complete the traceability cycle.

Once central records have this information, it should be possible, assuming the 'filing and finding' system is working satisfactorily, to trace such items 'in and out' as described for design control.

The action by quality assurance would be to verify the requirement for identification and traceability, and to audit the implementation of the system.

Handling and storage
All items received at the installation site should be stored and protected against misuse, damage and deterioration, and also controlled against unauthorised use.

Installation sites are generally very lax in this area and one particular industry which springs readily to mind is the building industry. A considerable amount of loss, damage and misuse occurs on building sites due, primarily, to the lack of control over handling and storage.

In cases where expensive and sophisticated equipment is concerned, time, effort and cost are expended to minimise loss, damage and misuse, yet the lesser valued items are generally left lying around. There is a saying that 'if one looks after the pennies, the pounds will take care of themselves'. This could apply to the construction site. The attitude in general is that as the materiel has been supplied by others, 'the others' should be responsible for it. Not so! The requirement to control purchaser-supplied materiel is quite specific.

The systems to control handling and storage are generally as described for manufacturing control.

The action by quality assurance should be to verify the establishment of the appropriate handling and storage system, and to audit implementation.

Special processes
The installation site, having received the purchaser-supplied materiel and any locally purchased items, will now have to translate all this into a finished and fit for purpose product. Special processes are paramount in this operation.

If one looks at the special processes listed for manufacturing control it should be apparent that these, and others, can be applicable to all manner of installation and construction site situations. Commissioning activities also utilise special processes. The purging of piping and vessel installations and the sealing to prevent ingress of moisture before actual 'switch-on' is one example.

In addition to those already mentioned, the British Standard 4778 also lists certain applications of forming, plastics and wood fabrication.

Company or site management should verify, therefore, which installation processes fall into the special category and determine methods of control, maintenance and calibration of special process equipment.

The suitability of personnel performing these special processes should also be established and should include the methods of evaluation. Instructions should be available to determine training and qualification requirements, and the updating and maintenance of qualifications by either periodic examination or continuous satisfactory performance.

The action by quality assurance would be: to verify the establishment of special process procedures; to audit the implementation and effectiveness of, and adherence to, such procedures and to verify the utilisation of appropriately trained and qualified personnel.

Non-conforming items or processes
In the installation and commissioning phases an inspection activity can uncover an unsatisfactory condition. Whenever such an unsatisfactory condition is found, there should be a system to direct personnel in the action to be taken. A method of identification should be utilised, such as that described in 'Identification of inspection status'.

During installation, it may not be possible to segregate the non-conforming item (if it is an item), and therefore a clear identification of the non-conformance should be clearly visible. The action to be taken in such circumstances will follow the same pattern as for manufacturing control.

The action by quality assurance should be to verify that a system for identifying and dispositioning non-conforming items, or processes, is established and to monitor, as required, its implementation and effectiveness.

Records
As for manufacturing, a system should be established to control the records generated during the installation and commissioning activities.

In the case of large projects, these records will, in all probability, be maintained at the construction site and handed over to the customer, or back to the central document control area on completion of activities.

In all other cases, the installer would return the records to his employer for filing.

The action by quality assurance should be to verify the establishment, where required, of a site-controlled record system and to monitor, by audit, the implementation and effectiveness of the system.

Where records are returned to a central document control area by the installer, then quality assurance should monitor, as required, to verify that such records are returned and filed as the system dictates.

Training
The subject of training in the installation phase has been touched upon already in special processes. There are other areas of activity which should require training of personnel and these are detailed in manufacturing control.

Site management should determine those activities which are to be covered by training needs. These training needs should be documented, together with the methods for training, and the documentation required to verify satisfactory completion of training. The frequency for updating training qualifications should be also established, as well as requirements for retraining in the event of poor performance or non-participation in an activity.

The action by quality assurance should be: to verify the establishment of a training policy and to monitor, by audit, that the requirements of such a policy are being implemented throughout; to verify that installation and commissioning personnel are receiving, or have received, the training as required and that the records of such training, or retraining, are maintained and updated.

Audit and corrective action

The quality assurance department would verify, initially, the establishment of procedures to control all installation and commissioning activities, and then monitor, by audit, their implementation, adherence and effectiveness.

As before, all non-conformances exposed during audits should be addressed by corrective action requests upon the appropriate party, with follow-up action to verify that corrective action had been taken and steps taken to prevent a recurrence of the deficiency.

Installation and commissioning are complete and the entire plant, facility or whatever is handed over to the customer in a fit for purpose condition .

MAINTENANCE

Maintenance of the unit will be periodically necessary if the unit is to continue to perform satisfactorily during its anticipated service life.

The requirements for maintenance should have been established during the design stage.

A programme for maintenance should be documented and here again most, if not all, of the activities described in this chapter from planning to audit and corrective action will be just as applicable to maintenance (particularly of major capital equipment and plant).

Audit and corrective action has been mentioned many times as being the means of verifying the implementation and effectiveness of, and adherence to, the documented quality programme.

The next act in the total presentation is to establish exactly what an audit is, and what it entails.

15

Audit and corrective action

Once a quality assurance programme has been developed and implemented the only possible way an organisation can verify its effectiveness is to carry out regular audits.

THE RESPONSIBILITY FOR AUDITING

Throughout all of the activities so far dealt with, it has been emphasised that one of the responsibilities of the quality assurance department is to undertake such audits.

In the very small organisation, the responsibility for auditing may rest with the senior executive himself. After all, as has been said many times, the senior executive has the ultimate responsibility for quality and the quality systems have been established by him, in conjunction with his senior management, and therefore he should be aware of the efficiency of his organisation.

There is a requirement for a company to be aware of its financial status and an audit is carried out to verify that a company's accounting system is in order and that the results are accurate.

With a financial audit, however, this is undertaken as a legal requirement under the Companies Act. The results do identify a company's profit and loss position and a company's board of directors will act on the results. The 'bottom line' is the spur.

WHY AUDIT?

A company's quality programme is not generally seen in the same light as the financial accounting system, yet, because of inefficient control over all its activities, a company could well be losing a great deal of money. The inefficiencies due to duplication of activities, high repair and scrap rates, malpractices and so on, may result in the quality costs (the costs of putting things right) being higher than the overall profit margin.

A quality audit, if effectively undertaken, should uncover such problems, providing the audit is carried out against documented requirements.

WHAT IS AN AUDIT?

All the quality assurance standards call up a requirement for the auditing or the review of the quality programme or plan, and, in general, such an activity could be defined as:

> A planned and documented activity performed in accordance with written procedures and check-lists to verify by investigation, and the examination and evaluation of objective evidence, that applicable elements of a quality programme or plan have been developed, documented and effectively implemented in accordance with specified requirements.

(The above definition has been developed with reference to BS 5882 and ANSI/ASME.NQA1 supplement S-1).

TYPES, DEPTHS AND SCOPE

As has already been stated, there is a requirement to seek objective evidence that an activity has been carried out in accordance with specified requirements. These specified requirements are the procedures and work instructions. Initially, however, immediately after the implementation of a quality programme, or plan, an audit should be carried out to confirm that all the relevant procedures and instructions are available at the activity locations, and that personnel are aware of their responsibilities within the programme or plan. In project-related industries, this would be undertaken at the commencement of each project. The objectives of such an audit are to confirm the existence of the necessary quality systems. Such an audit is known generally as a systems audit.

In order to appreciate this more fully, a case study is worth considering. A contractor was awarded a contract for the design of a major piece of equipment. The controls to be implemented for this contract were outlined in the project quality manual and comprised the following:

Contract review
Documentation preparation control and retention
Discipline check
Interdiscipline check
Internal design review
Design interface control
Change control
External design review
Audit

The contract included the requirements for a systems audit to be carried out within three weeks of contract start-up to confirm the existence of the necesary controls. The systems audit assessed whether or not the quality plan was adequate to meet the needs of the project. It also served to verify that the project personnel were aware of the requirements of the quality plan and that the procedures were available at the activity locations, but the systems audit did not verify whether the procedures were actually being complied with.

Depth of audit

The systems audit is, therefore, a superficial or 'shallow' audit and can be utilised very effectively to get the 'feel' of a quality programme or plan.

In order to confirm whether or not a procedure or work instruction is actually being implemented, an 'adherence' or 'compliance' audit is carried out. This 'adherence' or 'compliance' audit is a 'deep' audit. It gets down to the nitty-gritty so to speak.

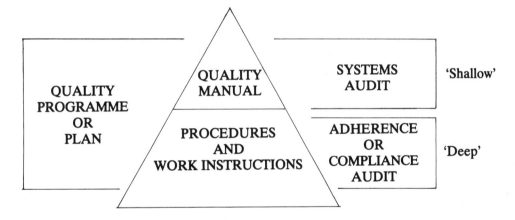

Scope of audit

The 'scope' of an audit relates to the amount of the quality assurance programme or plan that should be reviewed to confirm that the activities are in compliance with requirements.

Type of audit

It will have been noted in previous chapters that the quality assurance function covers not only the auditing of a company's own quality systems but, in the case of control of purchased materiel and services, the assessment and auditing of a supplier's quality systems. There are, therefore, two types of audit: internal and external. This chapter will deal in a general way with internal auditing only. For a more detailed examination of the subject related to both the internal auditing of a company's own management systems and those of its suppliers, the author recommends *Management Audits* by Allan J. Sayle, details of which are appended in the bibliography.

PREPARATION AND PLANNING

Audits, like all other activities, require preparation and planning and there are a number of steps to be considered:

(1) Compile the audit schedule.
(2) Notify the person or department to be audited (auditee).
(3) Identify, obtain and review all documentation relative to the audit.
(4) Develop the check-list.
(5) Agree the audit timetable.

A review of each of these steps is to be considered in detail.

The Audit Schedule

This should be established as soon as possible after a quality programme or plan is implemented. It is recommended that a systems audit be undertaken within four to six weeks of implementation and then compliance audits scheduled to commence immediately thereafter. The systems audit should identify areas of concern which could be used to establish priorities for future audits.

A typical audit schedule is given as Fig. 15.1. Once the timetable has been agreed, the arrangements can be made to carry out the audits.

Notify the Auditee

This should be done in writing with at least seven days notice of the intention to conduct an audit. Initially, the auditor (or team leader in the case of major audits) should informally contact the auditee(s) to agree a mutually convenient date and to discuss the audit scope, but confirmation of all such discussions should be made in writing. The notification would normally be in the form of an internal memo and should include the following information:

> Date and time of audit
> Audit scope
> Name(s) of auditor(s)
> Request to advise if date and time should not be convenient

Having made the formal notification, then all relevant information relating to the activities or functions to be audited should be obtained.

Identify, Obtain and Review all documentation relative to the Audit

This refers to documents such as procedures, work instructions, inspection and test plans, specifications, and so on. If a previous audit has already been carried out, then the previous audit report should form part of this documentation. There may be corrective actions still outstanding which should be followed up. Once all relevant information has been reviewed the next step should be to:

Develop an Audit Check-list

A check-list is not a mandatory exercise but it is strongly recommended. In developing a check-list, the auditor would be required to read all the relevant documents in depth. This should then make the auditor familiar with the auditee's activities, which would lead therefore to a greater understanding between the two parties. A check-list also acts as an *aide-mémoire* and governs the continuity and depth of the audit.

Many organisations utilise standard pre-prepared check-lists but the use of these generally results in the audit becoming a mechanical exercise on the part of the auditor, with the auditee becoming little more than an answering machine.

Check-lists should be developed utilising the system or procedural criteria. As has been mentioned, the procedural documents, if established to an agreed format, should be auditable documents and would readily lend themselves to check-list development. An example of a typical check-list is given in Fig. 15.2.

Continuing with the case history given on page 45 relating to the design contract, the check-list developed for that systems audit is given in Figs. 15.3a to 15.3e.

When developing check-lists for the audit of procedural activities (the adherence or compliance audit) care should be taken not to include items which would not produce objective evidence.

The procedure for auditing should give the auditor the flexibility to determine whether an activity is acceptable or not rather than a strict YES or NO. There are some instances where an activity may not be strictly in accordance with procedure but may otherwise be perfectly acceptable. It is, therefore, prudent to denote acceptability and qualify the result.

Once the check-lists have been developed, the next step is to:

Agree the audit timetable

This should be done in conjunction with the auditee. The timetable should be planned to be most effective and to avoid involving too many people. It is considered good practice to plan to commence audit proceedings at least half an hour after the auditee's commencement of work. This gives time for the auditee to prepare for the day's work and to allocate responsibilities to those not involved in the audit.

A late finish should be avoided where possible, as the auditee could have other pressing matters to attend to, the concern for which may make the auditee less attentive to the audit.

PERFORMANCE OF THE AUDIT

Upon arrival at the audit venue, the auditor (or audit team leader) should convene a brief meeting between the auditor and the auditee(s). This meeting is given many titles, such as entry meeting, entry interview, pre-audit meeting or opening meeting.

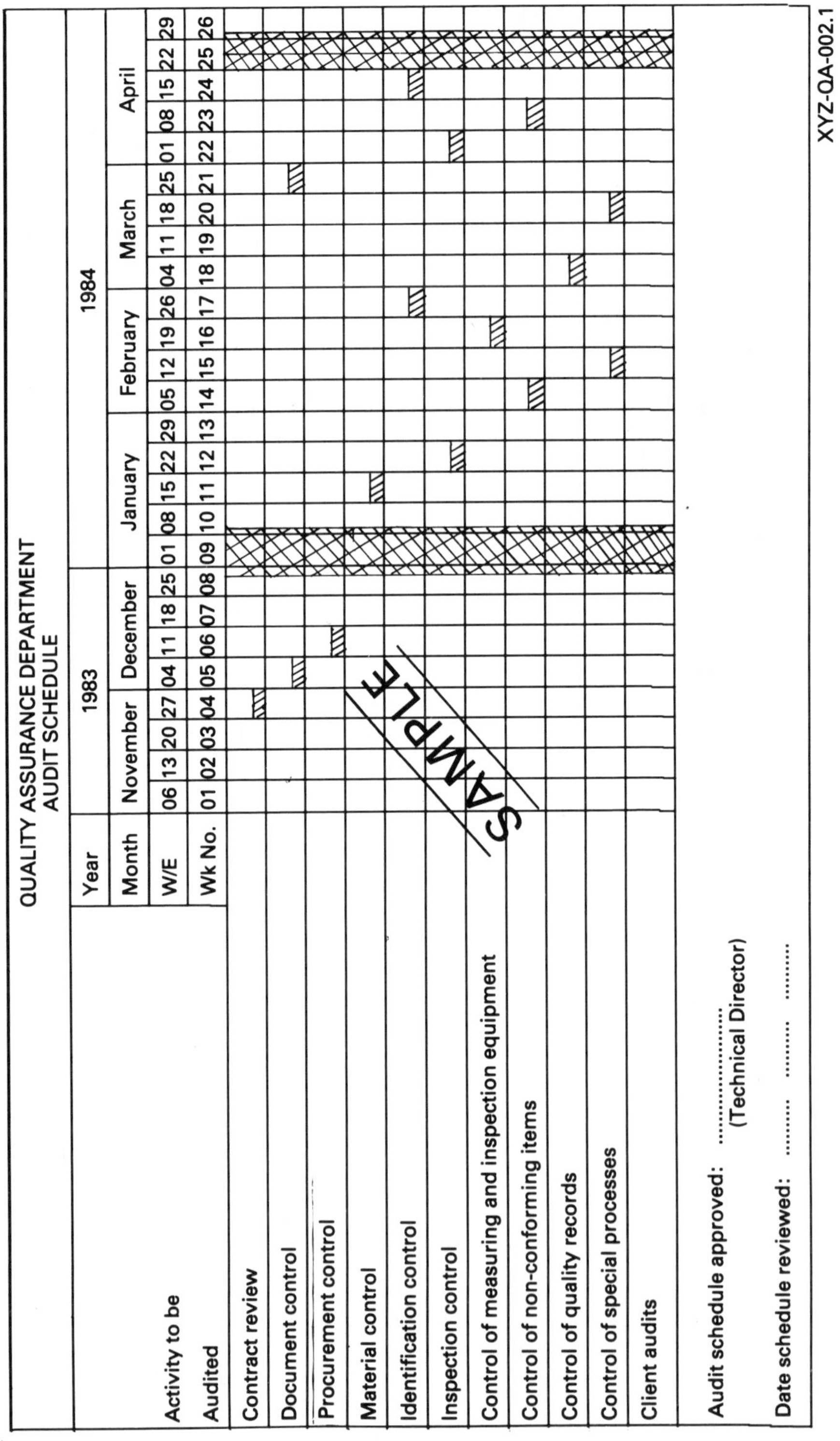

Fig. 15.1 — Audit schedule.

ITEM NO.	REQUIREMENT	ACTIVITY COMPLIANCE	COMMENTS/REMARKS

CHECK LIST FOR AUDIT REPORT NO.   Page   of

XYZ-QA-002.2

Fig. 15.2 — Audit check-list.

ITEM NO.	REQUIREMENT	ACTIVITY COMPLIANCE	COMMENTS/REMARKS
	CHECK LIST FOR AUDIT REPORT NO.		Page 1 of 5
1.	DESIGN CONTROL Is A QA Manual available and approved? 1.1 Are copies controlled? 1.2 Are copies latest revision? 1.3 Are all disciplines aware of their responsibilities within the Manual?		
2.	Does the organisational structure define quality responsibilities and authority? 2.1 Does this authority operate in practice?		
3.	Was contract review carried out? 3.1 Was action log maintained for missing/ambiguous information? 3.2 Have queries been actioned and closed out?		

XYZ-QA-002.2

Fig. 15.3a — Audit check-list—completed.

ITEM NO.	REQUIREMENT	CHECK LIST FOR AUDIT REPORT NO.	
		ACTIVITY COMPLIANCE	COMMENTS/REMARKS
4.	Has contact been made with Certifying Authority to establish certification requirements? 4.1 Is the procedure approved and in operation?		
5.	Is an adequate documentation control procedure in operation? 5.1 Is the procedure approved? 5.2 Does the procedure: 5.2.1 Ensure uniform presentation? 5.2.2 Detail identification requirements 5.2.3 Detail distribution requirements?		
6.	Is a discipline check procedure approved and in operation? 6.1 Are all disciplines aware of their responsibilities within the procedure? 6.2 Is the procedure auditable? 6.3 When was the last audit carried out?		

Page 2 of 5

XYZ-QA-002.2

Fig. 15.3b — Audit check-list—completed.

ITEM NO.	REQUIREMENT	ACTIVITY COMPLIANCE	COMMENTS/REMARKS
	CHECK LIST FOR AUDIT REPORT NO.		Page 3 of 5
7.	Is an inter-discipline check procedure available and approved? 7.1 Are all disciplines aware of their responsibilities within the procedure? 7.2 Is the procedure auditable? 7.3 When was the last audit carried out?		
8.	Is there facility within the project schedule for internal design reviews? 8.1 Is the procedure approved and in operation? 8.2 Is the responsibility defined for initiating reviews? 8.3 Is there facility for follow-up of comments? 8.4 Has a review yet been carried out? 8.4.1 Comments closed out?		
9.	Is there evidence of design interface control in operation? 9.1 Is the procedure available? 9.2 Is the procedure approved?		

XYZ-QA-002.2

Fig. 15.3c — Audit check-list—completed.

CHECK LIST FOR AUDIT REPORT NO.		Page 4 of 5
ITEM NO.	REQUIREMENT	ACTIVITY COMPLIANCE	COMMENTS/REMARKS
10.	Is a change control procedure available? 10.1 Is the procedure approved? 10.2 Are all disciplines aware of their responsibilities? 10.3 Is the procedure auditable? 10.4 When was the last audit carried out?		
11.	Is there facility within the project schedules for external design reviews? 11.1 Procedure? 11.2 Is the responsibility defined for initiating reviews? 11.3 Is there facility for follow up of comments? 11.4 Has a review yet been carried out? 11.4.1 Comments closed out?		

XYZ-QA-002.2

Fig. 15.3d — Audit check-list—completed.

ITEM NO.	REQUIREMENT	ACTIVITY COMPLIANCE	COMMENTS/REMARKS
12.	Is there corrective action procedure? 12.1 Is the procedure approved? 12.2 Are corrective measures taken when a non-conformance is observed? 12.3 Is the QA Manager advised of all non-conformances? 12.4 Is corrective action documented? 12.5 Does management review the status of the system?		

CHECK LIST FOR AUDIT REPORT NO.

Page 5 of 5

XYZ-QA-002.2

Fig. 15.3e — Audit check-list—completed.

The entry meeting

The purpose of an entry meeting is to:

— Introduce the auditor (or audit team) to the representatives of the auditee(s), if they are not already known to each other.
— Confirm briefly the purpose and scope of the audit.
— Review the audit scope, timetable and agenda.
— Agree a tentative time for a closing meeting.
— Arrange for escorts to accompany the auditor(s).

At this meeting, the auditor (or audit team leader) should record the names of those present.

The audit

The audit should be conducted using the prepared check-lists as a guide. These check-lists could be expanded, if necessary, to determine compliance with specified requirements and/or determine the effectiveness of the implementation of a system's element.

Objective evidence should be examined and details recorded on the check-list. All essential information, for example, identification of the evidence examined, specific details of non-conforming or adverse conditions, together with any applicable references, should also be recorded.

In completing the audit check-list under the heading 'Activity compliance', the auditor should state 'yes', 'acceptable', 'not acceptable', 'no', 'not applicable' (N/A) or 'see comment'. The 'Comments/remarks' column is used to expand on the activity or to reference non-conformances and objective evidence.

Upon completion of the audit, and before the closing meeting, the audit team (if more than one auditor is present) should meet to evaluate the evidence generated during the audit. The team should analyse any apparent non-conformances or adverse conditions to ensure validity as audit findings. Objective evidence of a departure from approved procedures, documented requirements and/or other applicable documents should be considered as valid justification for an audit finding. Such audit findings should be recorded and a document known as a corrective action request (CAR) form is a typical vehicle for this. An example is given in Fig. 15.4.

Completing the corrective action request form

The corrective action request form should be completed by the auditor to show only the nature of the non-conformance. The sections for 'Corrective action', 'Action taken to prevent recurrence of non-conformance' and 'Follow-up and close out' should be left blank at this stage.

Having reviewed the audit findings and completed the CAR forms where necessary, the auditor (or audit team leader) should convene a meeting with the auditee(s) to discuss the outcome of the audit. This meeting, like the entry meeting, is given many titles, such as closing meeting, exit meeting, exit interview, post-audit meeting, and others.

XYZ COMPANY	CORRECTIVE ACTION REQUEST	CAR No.
COMPANY/DEPARTMENT/DISCIPLINE AUDITED ADDRESS:		AUDIT No. DATE OF AUDIT
BASIS OF AUDIT: QA REQUIREMENTS FOR		
AUDITOR:	COMPANY/DEPARTMENT/ DISCIPLINE REPRESENTATIVE	AREA AUDITED:
NON-CONFORMANCE SIGNATURE........................ SIGNATURE................. (COMPANY/DEPARTMENT/DISCIPLINE REPRESENTATIVE) AUDITOR		
CORRECTIVE ACTION DATE FOR COMPLETION OF CORRECTIVE ACTION SIGNATURE........................ DATE:- (COMPANY/DEPARTMENT/DISCIPLINE REPRESENTATIVE)		
ACTION TAKEN TO PREVENT RECURRENCE OF NON-CONFORMANCE DATE FOR COMPLETION OF ACTION TO PREVENT RECURRENCE SIGNATURE........................ DATE:- (COMPANY/DEPARTMENT/DISCIPLINE REPRESENTATIVE)		
FOLLOW-UP AND CLOSE OUT PROPOSED FOLLOW-UP DATE:- FOLLOW-UP DETAILS CAR CLOSE OUT DATE SIGNATURE................... AUDITOR		

XYZ-QA-004.1

Fig. 15.4 — Corrective action request.

The exit meeting

At this meeting should be present the auditee(s) and, as necessary, management representatives. The auditor (or audit team leader) should again record the names of all persons attending the meeting.

During this meeting, the auditor (or team leader) should present an overview of the audit results and should present any findings, and should ensure that such findings are understood by the auditee(s). At this stage the CARs (if any) should be presented to the auditee(s) and the auditee requested to sign the first section of the form to indicate his understanding of the non-conformance. The signature does not indicate an agreement, only an acknowledgement. A copy of each CAR is left with the auditee.

The auditor (or team leader) should advise the auditee(s) of the intended issue date of the formal audit report and should request that the auditee(s) acknowledge receipt of the report within an agreed time. Acknowledgement of the report should include the expected date of the completion of the action to rectify the deficiency and to prevent recurrence.

The audit report should include the formal issue of the corrective action requests on which the auditee would indicate, in the appropriate sections, the corrective action taken and the action taken to prevent recurrence. It could well be that the corrective action taken will also prevent recurrence, in which case it should be so stated.

THE AUDIT REPORT

Audit reports, as for any other series of documents, should be presented in a uniform manner and the formulation of such covered by procedure. A typical audit report would comprise the following:

Lead (or cover) sheet (Fig. 15.5)
Report sheet (Fig. 15.6)
Corrective action requests

and, if so required, the completed check-lists could be included. This practice, however, is not recommended as it only adds to the amount of paper distributed. The completed check-lists should be filed with a copy of the audit report and made available for the auditee's review when necessary.

The results of the audit should be summarised on the lead sheet and any audit findings (CARs) should be itemised. By giving a summary on the first page this enables management to see at a glance the outcome of the audit. If further information is required then reference can be made to the details in the body of the report.

An audit summary could read as follows:

Summary of audit

The purpose of this audit was to verify the implementation of document control, as covered by procedure Nos. XYZ-DOC-005, 007 and 008. The audit indicated that generally the requirements of the

XYZ COMPANY	AUDIT REPORT (LEAD SHEET)	AUDIT REPORT No. PAGE 1 OF
AUDITED ORGANISATION	PROJECT/PURCHASE ORDER No.	
	SCOPE OF SUPPLY	
ADDRESS		
	TYPE OF AUDIT DATE OF AUDIT	
TELEPHONE No.	AUDIT CRITERIA	
TELEX No.	AUDIT TEAM	
PERSONS CONTACTED		
	PREVIOUS AUDIT DATE	
	PREVIOUS AUDIT REFERENCE	
SUMMARY OF AUDIT		
SIGNATURE.............. (AUDIT TEAM LEADER) DATE:-	SIGNATURE............... (QUALITY MANAGER) DATE:-	

XYZ-QA-002.3

Fig. 15.5 — Audit report lead sheet.

XYZ COMPANY	AUDIT REPORT	AUDIT REPORT No. PAGE OF

XYZ-QA-002.4

Fig. 15.6 — Audit report sheet.

procedures were being implemented but there were certain areas which would appear to require much closer attention.

Deficiencies were identified with regard to the delegation of responsibility, the control of document distribution, the review of documentation and maintaining records up to date.

These deficiences have been addressed by a total of six corrective action requests, Nos. 001–006 inclusive.

The body of the report should follow a prescribed format and, as an example, should report on:

The entry meeting
The audit itself
The exit meeting
Designated follow-up
General observations

Each heading, if this format is used, should always appear in the report and when a heading is not applicable the words 'not applicable' should follow beneath the heading. To explain this more fully:

Entry meeting
Provide a brief summary of the meeting, stating who attended. Avoid too much detail; entry meetings usually follow a very standard pattern. List any specific requests made and/or agreements reached with the auditee.

Audit
Give a detailed account of the audit, listing the areas which were found to be satisfactory and in compliance with requirements. Detail the areas which were not in compliance with requirements and which it was necessary to address by corrective action requests.

Include as 'observations of concern' areas which were deficient but which were not addressed by corrective action requests. If considered appropriate, make constructive 'recommendations' to the auditee for rectifying the deficiency but do not be dogmatic (auditees will usually find another way of correcting a deficiency in any case).

Exit meeting
Provide a brief summary of the meeting, stating who attended (as for entry meetings, avoid too much detail). Exit meetings usually follow a standard pattern. Record if any corrective action requests are withdrawn as a result of further discussion and additional information being provided at the exit meeting. Record if the auditee declined to sign a corrective action request (this will also be stated on the corrective action request form by the audit team leader).

Designated follow-up

State the intention to undertake a follow-up audit to verify close out of each corrective action request, usually within a defined period of the final date stated for the completion of corrective action, and the action to prevent recurrence of the identified deficiencies.

General observations

Include any general observations considered applicable and constructive. As an example:

> Although generally the requirements of the procedures were being implemented, more attention is required adequately to control document distribution, documentation review and the maintenance of up-to-date records.

If there are no 'general observations' add 'not applicable' beneath this heading.

When complete, the audit report should then be signed on the cover sheet by the auditor (or audit team leader) and by the appropriate supervisor (corporate quality assurance manager, chief engineer, etc.) after he has reviewed the report and the contents have his approval.

The original of any corrective action request raised as a result of the audit should accompany the audit report, which is then forwarded to the auditee.

It is sound professional practice to ensure that the audit report is completed and issued to the auditee, under a covering memo, within 14 days of the final date of the audit. The covering memo should identify the final date by which responses are required for the audit findings—corrective action requests.

THE FOLLOW-UP

Following receipt of the responses to the audit findings, the auditor (or audit team leader) should undertake follow-up activities, usually in the form of another audit, to verify the completion of the action to correct the deficiency and the action taken to prevent recurrence.

If the follow-up indicates that the actions taken have corrected the deficiency and prevented a recurrence of the deficiency, then the corrective action request can be closed out and this should be stated on the corrective action request form in the appropriate section.

If the follow-up indicates that the action taken does not correct the deficiency, then this should be stated on the corrective action request form and the deficiency reidentified by issuing a revision to the corrective action request.

It may be necessary, in the event of a continuing deficiency, for the auditor to call in support from senior management—hence the requirement of all quality assurance programme standards for such an organisational structure.

Audits, audit reports, corrective action requests and follow-up audits should be controlled and regulated. It is, therefore, prudent to establish and maintain details of all such activities. Fig. 15.7 is a typical example of an audit report status log, while Fig. 15.8 shows a typical example of a corrective action request status log.

THE AUDIT ROUTE

The complete auditing function has been set out in Fig. 15.9 in the form of a flow chart, which takes each activity step by step from the formulation of the quality programme through to implementation and adherence.

Each activity is identified with the appropriate responsible department and, where applicable, with the interfacing department.

Following the chart through from the establishment of the quality programme (a management responsibility), the procedures and instructions are developed and implemented by the appropriate departments. These procedures and instructions are then audited by the quality assurance department to confirm implementation and effectiveness. If compliant and effective, then the audit report is issued to confirm this. If non-compliant or ineffective, then corrective action requests should be issued on the department concerned, together with an audit report.

The department should then determine and implement corrective action and the action to prevent recurrence.

If the discrepancy had been a straightforward operator fault, then the action to correct the deficiency would follow the left-hand route on the flow chart. The follow-up audit would either confirm that the action taken to correct the deficiency and to prevent recurrence was satisfactory, in which case the corrective action request would be closed out, or the action taken was ineffective, in which case the corrective action request would be reissued.

The discrepancy may be due to a procedural fault. The activity may have been incorrectly documented—the activity itself being perfectly effective (this often occurs when procedures are written by personnel other than those who are familiar with the activity). In such a case an amendment to the procedure would be required. The revision would then be approved, issued and implemented. A follow-up audit would be carried out to confirm effectiveness, in which case the corrective action request would be closed out, or if still non-compliant or ineffective, then the corrective action request would be reissued or revised. Corrective action could go either way, depending on whether the procedure is still ineffective or whether the operator is at fault—thus completing the loop until eventual satisfactory implementation and close out.

THE AUDITOR—GUIDE, PHILOSOPHER AND FRIEND

Throughout the audit activity, particularly in the early stages of the implementation of quality systems, there are bound to be audit findings. Personnel may well have to get used to doing things differently and the new

AUDIT REPORT STATUS LOG

AUDIT REPORT NO:	AUDIT TYPE	AUDIT TEAM LEADER	AUDIT DATE	COMPANY/ DEPARTMENT/ DISCIPLINE AUDITED	PROCEDURES/ CRITERIA AUDITED	CONTRACT/ PURCHASE ORDER NO:	DATE AUDIT REPORT ISSUED	CAR's ISSUED

ZYX-QA-002.5

Fig. 15.7 — Audit report status log.

CORRECTIVE ACTION REQUEST (CAR) STATUS LOG

XYZ-OA-004.2

CAR SERIAL No.	CAR ISSUED To	DEFICIENCY	AUDIT DATE	INITIALS OF AUDITOR	RESPONSE DUE DATE	DATE REMINDER SENT	CORRECTIVE ACTION COMPLETION DATE	ACTION PREVENT RECURRENCE COMPLETION DATE	PROPOSED FOLLOW-UP DATE	DATE CAR CLOSED

Fig. 15.8 — CAR status log.

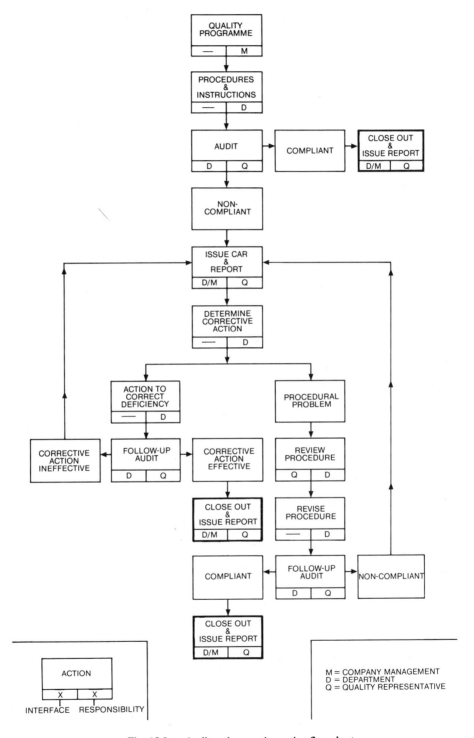

Fig. 15.9 — Audit and corrective action flow chart.

methods may be foreign to them. The auditor should not adopt a belligerent attitude but should be the guide, philosopher and friend. To adopt the so-called 'gotcher' mentality will lead only to antagonism and non-co-operation.

Should a deficiency be found and the auditor asked to make a recommendation regarding corrective action, then by all means assist in this respect but it is prudent to advise the auditee that the advice given is purely personal and should not be taken as 'gospel'. Wherever possible the auditee should be left to determine his own corrective action.

Experience has shown that recommending corrective action (particularly in the case of external audits) can create more problems than it solves. The recommended corrective action is invariably taken as an instruction and when the recommendation is found to be ineffective the auditor usually finds the blame laid at his door.

Corrective action, where a major deficiency is concerned, may involve the auditee in a great deal of time and money. In such instances should the auditee act upon a recommendation which is ineffective in its result, then the auditee may well be inclined to submit an invoice for the costs involved.

An auditor should be aware of the implications when recommending corrective action and should, therefore, be very sure of his ground. He must have experience with the activity under audit.

In many instances, particularly where auditors are inexperienced, the recommendation made when a non-compliant action is discovered is to amend the procedure. Amending the procedure is an easy let out. A follow-up audit by an experienced auditor usually uncovers the truth. The auditee hadn't read the procedure in the first place and was, therefore, not aware of the requirement. It is a management responsibility to make all personnel aware of their commitments.

Once a deficiency has been discovered and reported upon, it is worthwhile keeping in touch with the auditee to evaluate the progress of corrective action. This acts as a spur to the auditee and reminds him of his responsibilities. It could also highlight any problems which the auditee may be experiencing with regard to close out.

As well as being a guide, philosopher and friend, the auditor should also have many other attributes.

AUDITOR QUALIFICATION AND TRAINING

The audit has set out to examine the adequacy of the systems for assuring quality. Like a financial audit, we would expect the auditor to be qualified and experienced. A quality audit is not as simple as it may sound. The auditor must have the right background to perform the audit. He needs, apart from the appropriate technical or scientific training, a knowledge of:

— Quality assurance standards
— Quality practices of the industry concerned
— Contractual and regulatory requirements

— Planning
— Auditing practices

The majority of quality assurance standards stipulate that audits should be performed by qualified personnel who are not directly involved with the activity under audit.

Only one standard actually gives any guidance regarding the level of qualification and experience. The standard referred to is ANSI/ASME NQA-1 1983 edition. Within this standard are requirements for the qualification of quality assurance program audit personnel (supplement 2S-3) and non-mandatory guidance on the education and experience of lead auditors. These details are reproduced with the kind permission of the American Society of Mechanical Engineers as Figs. 15.10a to 15.10d.

In the UK a scheme for the registration of Lead Assessors of Quality Management Systems has been developed and is operated and administered by the Institute of Quality Assurance (IQA). This scheme is independent of any sectional interests.

The scheme is aimed, primarily, at assessments which are undertaken by purchasers and procurement bodies and should form part of a company's procedure for the control of purchased materiel and services.

The scheme identifies seven criteria for qualification and experience, and these requirements are reproduced with the kind permission of the Institute of Quality Assurance as Fig. 15.11.

The requirements of the IQA scheme and those of ANSI/ASME NQA-1 are similar and could be used to establish requirements for internal auditing capability.

SYSTEM OUTLINE

The audit activities and auditor qualification and training covered in this chapter are summed up in a typical system outline (Fig. 15.12), which could serve as part of a company's quality manual.

ANS1/ASME NQA–1–1983 Edition

SUPPLEMENT 2S-3
SUPPLEMENTARY REQUIREMENTS FOR THE QUALIFICATION OF
QUALITY ASSURANCE PROGRAM AUDIT PERSONNEL

1 GENERAL

This Supplement provides amplified requirements for the qualification of an audit team leader, henceforth identified as a *Lead Auditor*, who organizes and directs audits, reports audit findings, and evaluates corrective action. This Supplement also provides amplified requirements for the qualifications of individuals, henceforth referred to as *Auditors*, who participate in an audit, such as technical specialists, management representatives, and auditors-in-training. It supplements the requirements of Basic Requirement 2 of this Standard and shall be used in conjunction with that Basic Requirement when and to the extent specified by the organization invoking this Standard.

2 QUALIFICATION OF AUDITORS

2.1 Responsibility of Auditing Organization

The responsible auditing organization shall establish the audit personnel qualifications and the requirements for the use of technical specialists to accomplish the auditing of quality assurance programs. Personnel selected for quality assurance auditing assignments shall have experience or training commensurate with the scope, complexity, or special nature of the activities to be audited. Auditors shall have, or be given, appropriate training or orientation to develop their competence for performing required audits. Competence of personnel for performance of the various auditing functions shall be developed by one or more of the methods given in (a) through (c) below:

(a) Orientation to provide a working knowledge and understanding of this Standard and the auditing organization's procedures for implementing audits and reporting results;

(b) Training programs to provide general and specialized training in audit performance. General training shall include fundamentals, objectives, characteristics, organization, performance, and results of quality auditing. Specialized training shall include methods of examining, questioning, evaluating, and documenting specific audit items and methods of closing out audit findings.

(c) On-the-job training, guidance, and counseling under the direct supervision of a Lead Auditor. Such training shall include planning, performing, reporting, and follow-up action involved in conducting audits.

3 QUALIFICATION OF LEAD AUDITORS

An individual shall meet the requirements of 3.1 through 3.4 below prior to being designated a Lead Auditor.

3.1 Communication Skills

The prospective Lead Auditor shall have the capability to communicate effectively, both in writing and orally. These skills shall be attested to in writing by the Lead Auditor's employer.

3.2 Training

Prospective Lead Auditors shall have training to the extent necessary to assure their competence in auditing skills. Training in the following areas shall be given based upon management evaluation of the particular needs of each prospective Lead Auditor.

3.2.1 Knowledge and understanding of this Standard and other nuclear-related codes, standards, regulations, and regulatory guides, as applicable.

3.2.2 General structure of quality assurance programs as a whole and applicable elements as defined in this Standard.

3.2.3 Auditing techniques of examining, questioning, evaluating, and reporting; methods of identifying and following up on corrective action items; and closing out audit findings.

Fig. 15.10a — NQA requirements.

ANS1/ASME NQA–1–1983 Edition

3.2.4 Audit planning in the quality-related functions for the following activities: design, purchasing, fabrication, handling, shipping, storage, cleaning, erection, installation, inspection, testing, statistics, nondestructive examination, maintenance, repair, operation, modification of nuclear facilities or associated components, and safety aspects of the nuclear facility.

3.2.5 On-the-job training to include applicable elements of the audit program.

3.3 Audit participation

The prospective Lead Auditor shall have participated in a minimum of five (5) quality assurance audits within a period of time not to exceed three (3) years prior to the date of qualification, one audit of which shall be a nuclear quality assurance audit within the year prior to his qualification.

3.4 Examination

The prospective Lead Auditor shall pass an examination which shall evaluate his comprehension of and ability to apply the body of knowledge identified in 3.2 above. The test may be oral, written, practical, or any combination of the three types. The development and administration of the examination shall be in accordance with Section 5 of this Supplement.

4 MAINTENANCE OF QUALIFICATION

4.1 Maintenance of Proficiency

Lead Auditors shall maintain their proficiency through: regular and active participation in the audit process; review and study of codes, standards, procedures, instructions, and other documents related to quality assurance program and program auditing; and participation in training programs. Based on annual assessment, management may extend the qualification, require retraining, or require requalification. These evaluations shall be documented.

4.2 Requalification

Lead Auditors who fail to maintain their proficiency for a period of two years or more shall require requalification. Requalification shall include retraining in accordance with the requirements of 3.2 above, reexamination in accordance with 3.4 above, and participation as an Auditor in at least one nuclear quality assurance audit.

5 ADMINISTRATION

5.1 Organizational Responsibility

Training of auditors shall be the responsibility of the employer. The responsible auditing organization shall select and assign personnel who are independent of any direct responsibility for performance of the activities which they will audit. The Lead Auditor shall, prior to commencing the audit, concur that assigned personnel collectively have experience or training commensurate with the scope, complexity, or special nature of the activities to be audited.

5.2 Qualification Examination

The development and administration of the examination for a Lead Auditor required by 3.4 above is the responsibility of the employer. The employer may delegate this activity to an independent certifying agency, but shall retain responsibility for conformance of the examination and its administration to this Standard. Integrity of the examination shall be maintained by the employer or certifying agency through appropriate confidentiality of files and, where applicable, proctoring of examinations. Copies of the objective evidence regarding the type(s) and content of the examination(s) shall be retained by the employer in accordance with the requirements of Section 6 below.

6 RECORDS

6.1 General

Records of personnel qualifications for Auditors and Lead Auditors performing audits shall be established and maintained by the employer.

6.2 Certification and Qualification

Each Lead Auditor shall be certified by his employer as being qualified to lead audits. This certification shall, as a minimum, document the following:
(a) employer's name;
(b) Lead Auditor's name;
(c) date of certification or recertification;
(d) basis of qualification (i.e., education, experience, communication skills, training, examination, etc.);
(e) signature of employer's designated representative who is responsible for such certification.

6.3 Updating of Lead Auditor's Records

Records for each Lead Auditor shall be maintained and updated annually.

Fig. 15.10b — NQA requirements.

ANS1/ASME NQA–1–1983 Edition

APPENDIX 2A-3
NONMANDATORY GUIDANCE ON THE EDUCATION AND EXPERIENCE OF LEAD AUDITORS

1 GENERAL

This Appendix provides nonmandatory guidance relative to the education and experience which may be used for the qualification of Lead Auditors. This Appendix may be used in conjunction with Basic Requirement 2 and Supplement 2S-3.

2 EDUCATION AND EXPERIENCE

The prospective Lead Auditor should have verifiable evidence that a minimum of ten (10) credits under the following score system have been accumulated.

2.1 Education (4 Credits Maximum)

Associate degree from an accredited institution: score one (1) credit, or if the degree is in engineering, physical sciences, mathematics, or quality assurance, score two (2) credits; or

A bachelor's degree from an accredited institution: score two (2) credits, or if the degree is in engineering, physical sciences, mathematics, or quality assurance, score three (3) credits; in addition, score one (1) credit for a master's degree in engineering, physical sciences, business management, or quality assurance from an accredited institution.

2.2 Experience (9 Credits Maximum)

Technical experience in engineering, manufacturing, construction, operation, or maintenance: score one (1) credit for each full year with a maximum of five (5) credits for this aspect of experience.

If two (2) years of this experience have been in the nuclear field, score one (1) additional credit; or

If two (2) years of this experience have been in quality assurance, score two (2) additional credits; or

If two (2) years of this experience have been in auditing, score three (3) additional credits; or

If two (2) years of this experience have been in nuclear quality assurance, score three (3) additional credits; or

If two (2) years of this experience have been in nuclear quality assurance auditing, score four (4) additional credits.

2.3 Other Credentials of Professional Competence
(2 Credits Maximum)

For certification of competency in engineering, science, or quality assurance specialties issued and approved by a State Agency or National Professional or Technical Society: score two (2) credits.

2.4 Rights of Management (2 Credits Maximum)

The Lead Auditor's employer may grant up to two (2) credits for other performance factors applicable to auditing which may not be explicitly called out in this Appendix. Examples of these factors are leadership, sound judgment, maturity, analytical ability, tenacity, past performance, and quality assurance training courses.

3 RECORDS

The sample form shown in Fig. 2A-3.1 is provided for utilization as a record of Lead Auditor qualification.

Fig. 15.10c — NQA requirements.

FIG. 2A-3.1 SAMPLE FORM FOR RECORD OF LEAD AUDITOR QUALIFICATION

RECORD OF LEAD AUDITOR QUALIFICATION	Name	Date
EMPLOYER:		

QUALIFICATION POINT REQUIREMENTS		CREDITS
Education—University/Degree Date	4 Credits Max.	_____
1. Undergraduate Level 2. Graduate Level		
Experience — Company/Dates	9 Credits Max.	_____
Technical (0–5 credits) and Nuclear Industry (0–1 credit), or Quality Assurance (0–2 credits), or Auditing (0–4 credits)		
Professional Accomplishment — Certificate/Date	2 Credits Max.	_____
1. P.E. 2. Society		
Management — Justification/ Evaluator/Date	2 Credits Max.	_____
Explain: Evaluated by: (Name and Title)	_____ Date	
	Total Credits:	_____

AUDIT COMMUNICATION SKILLS
Evaulated by: (Name and Title)   _____ Date:

AUDIT TRAINING COURSES		Date
Course Title or Topic: 1. 2.		

AUDIT PARTICIPATION			
	Location	Audit	Date
1.			
2.			
3.			
4.			
5.			

EXAMINATION:	PASSED:	DATE:

AUDITOR QUALIFICATION CERTIFIED BY: (Signature and Title)		Date Certified		
ANNUAL EVALUATION				
(Signature and Date)				

Fig. 15.10d — NQA requirements.

INSTITUTE OF QUALITY ASSURANCE

Qualification and experience requirements for quality assurance management systems lead assessors

1. Organisation or individuals applying for registration of Lead Assessors, shall be able to demonstrate that nominees meet the following requirements:-

   (a) They should be academically qualified in both a recognised scientific/technological discipline (e.g. Engineering, Pharmacy, Chemistry, etc.,) and in quality assurance. For guidance, the following is a non-exclusive list of acceptable qualifications:-

       Scientific/Technological:
       A suitable degree, C.Eng. or HNC/HND.

       Quality Assurance:
       The academic level and practical experience required for Corporate membership of Institute of Quality Assurance;

   (b) Have satisfactorily completed a training course in quality assurance management system assessment recognised by the Management Board and have satisfied any examination or test of competence embodied in the course;

   (c) Have had a minimum of five years recent and relevant practical experience, of which at least three years have been devoted to the application of quality assurance principles;

   (d) Have taken part within three years immediately prior to application, as a member of a quality assurance management system assessment team, in assessments of at least five companies, to the satisfaction of the assessment organisation. Such assessments must have been to BS 5750 Parts 1 or 2, or the equivalent standards of a major purchasing organisation;

   (e) Have competent working knowledge of nationally-recognised quality assurance management system assessment standards;

   (f) Have the necessary personal qualities of integrity, tact and character to perform the duties of a Lead Assessor;

   (g) Have confirmed willingness to accept and abide by the Code of Conduct laid down by the Institute of Quality Assurance and set out in Appendix B to this document.

Note:
These requirements pertain to the situation existing at 1 November 1985 and may be subject to change after that date.

Fig. 15.11 — Institute of Quality Assurance Lead Assessor scheme.

Typical system outline for quality assurance audits

1.0 The XYZ Company shall implement and operate a system which shall adequately evaluate the implementation and effectiveness of, and the adherence to, the documented quality assurance programme.

   1.1 The Quality Manager shall establish, document and implement a plan for audits which shall objectively evaluate the adequacy and implementation of the XYZ Company quality programme.

   1.2 The audit plan shall define:

      1.2.1 The activities, systems or procedures to be audited.

      1.2.2 Those personnel qualified to perform audits.

      1.2.3 Frequency of audits.

      1.2.4 Methods of reporting findings and recommendations.

      1.2.5 The means for having corrective actions agreed upon and implemented.

   1.3 Audits shall include an evaluation of:

      1.3.1 Activities, processes, work areas, items and services being produced.

      1.3.2 Quality practices, systems, procedures and instructions.

      1.3.3 Certification, documents and records.

   1.4 Audits shall be carried out by appropriately trained personnel who are not directly responsible for the area being audited.

   1.5 Audits shall be performed in accordance with documented audit procedures and/or check-lists which identify essential characteristics.

   1.6 Management responsible for the area audited shall review, agree and correct deficiences revealed in the documented audit results.

   1.7 All action taken to correct deficiences shall be re-audited to verify compliance and a close out report issued.

   1.8 Details of WHO, WHAT and HOW are defined in XYZ Company written procedures and work instructions.

Fig. 15.12 — Typical system outline for quality assurance audit.

16

An introduction to computer software control

With computer-aided design (CAD) becoming more and more common-place, the ability to assure the quality of the related software has presented, and indeed is still presenting, many problems. It is worthwhile, therefore, taking a brief look into the subject, if only to verify how closely computer software control relates to design control, as discussed in Chapter 11.

WHAT IS SOFTWARE?

A start should be made by defining what software is. The *Penguin Dictionary of Computers* defines it as follows:

> In its most general form, software is a term used in contrast to hardware to refer to all programs which can be used on a particular computer system.

(In computer software parlance, 'program' rather than 'programme' is used.)
It is, therefore, an intangible item representing information stored on disc, tape or punched card.

Software systems may be more easily understood if looked upon as containing a number of communicating processes which run independently of one another. Each independent communication process represents a single activity.

THE COMMUNICATING PROCESSES

The software design activity identifies, integrates and co-ordinates these various communicating processes by means of selection. The selection of such processes is determined by the application i.e. design, document control, data storage, etc. The more processes which are selected, the more interfaces are involved.

To explain this more fully it is worthwhile extending the Wagnerian philosophy of *Gesamtkunstwerk* still further. After the initial planning of the total presentation of the music drama, it is then written down, or designed, by the composer. Wagner would have written the orchestral part on the musical score. The vocal parts would be written within the appropriate section of the score.

Instructions would have also been documented by him regarding the costumes and the scenery. In all, there are four communicating processes involved in *Gesamtkunstwerk:* music, voice, costume and scenery. All of these need to be brought together so that the final result is what the composer intended.

It is the bringing together of these four art forms at the right place and at the right time which compares with the interfacing of the communicating processes in software design. These software interfaces must be designed to occur also at the right place at the right time if the desired result (or fitness for purpose of the software design) is to be achieved. It is the initial planning and eventual control of these interfaces which are fundamental to software design.

Assuming the music drama is to be transferred to video tape from an actual performance, then the performance must be fault-free (or as near fault-free as possible) if the recording is to be acceptable. This means that the composer's interpretation of the orchestral and vocal scores must be understood by the conductor.

Scenery and costume details are easily documented and would be quite easily interpreted.

Once the video recording is made, it is too late to change any details, unless those sections requiring change are re-enacted, rerecorded and edited into the original tape. In order to do this, the changes should be documented, or identified, in the score.

The same thing applies to computer software. Changes should be documented.

Inspection of a piece of hardware has always been possible to verify conformance to a given requirement or specification, even though at the time of inspection the hardware may have been unsuitable for service requirements. For software, however, there is nothing to inspect because, as has already been said, it is invariably in the form of information stored on a magnetic tape or disc.

If there is nothing to inspect, then the only assurance of quality is with the selection, integration and interfacing of the processes themselves.

As with design control, software control requirements will be seen to be very similar.

The computer industry is a rapidly expanding industry. The hardware manufacturers are many and varied, and software languages are just as numerous. The computer differs enormously from other man-made items in its versatility in coping with countless applications.

SOFTWARE LANGUAGES

These various applications are generally tied to software design techniques which are known as languages. Most languages are identified by their acronyms and, as an example, a few languages are identified to give an idea of the variations:

FORTRAN — FORmula TRANslation. A language for scientific and mathematical applications.

ALGOL — Originally known as IAL or International Algebraic Language. It is the European equivalent to Fortran which was developed in the USA at the same time.

BASIC — Beginner All-purpose Symbolic Code. A high-level language principally designed for developing programs in conversational mode.

COBOL — COmmon Business Oriented Language. A language internationally accepted for general commercial use.

and so on.

With all these languages and the associated hardware, it is imperative that the user specifies exactly what the requirements are. These requirements should be specified in basic terms and the software design engineers will then translate them into the appropriate design technique.

THE MAJOR ACTIVITIES

Upon receiving the software requirement or contract, it is therefore most necessary to review the requirements in detail.

Referring to the table in design control (Fig. 11.1), the first activity will be found to be contract review. It goes without saying that this is an equally, if not more, important activity for software quality assurance.

Contract review (planning)

This activity is identical to that for design control and will require the establishment of a review team to consider, in detail, the customer requirements and to verify a complete understanding of the software applications.

A quality plan should be developed in a manner described in Chapter 9 and should detail the procedural controls to cover the contract requirements. These controls should include as a minimum:

Document preparation, control and retention
Discipline check
Interdiscipline check
Internal design review
Change control
External design review
Audit and corrective action

The action by quality assurance should be to verify, either by attendance at or by the evidence of minutes, that the contract review meeting was carried out and that actions arising from the meeting were satisfactorily closed out.

Document preparation, control and retention
Initially, the software design requirements and applications will be documented and the methods of preparation, checking, approval and distribution are the same as for hardware design.

The method of documenting software design activities should be agreed, defined and communicated to all concerned.

Documentation identification should be standardised and controlled and should include any customer requirements.

Document approval procedures should be established and the appropriate approval responsibilities (signatories) registered.

Document checking routines, including the routines for amending documents, should be formalised.

Document issue and distribution should be controlled on the 'need to know' basis with a formal reproduction system as described in Chapter 11.

In addition to standard design documentation, there will be the requirement for a software system manual, programmer's and operator's manuals, specifications for tests and trials, and so on. All such documents should be covered by formal controls, which will ensure that the format and contents of the documents are in accordance with contract requirements.

The methods of retaining documents during design activities, together with retrieval methods, storage facilities and eventual handover to the customer, should be established.

The action by quality assurance would be to verify the formulation of all necessary procedures to cover the document control activities and to confirm implementation and the effectiveness of the document control system.

Discipline and interdiscipline checking:
These should follow the same pattern as that described in Chapter 11.

Internal design reviews
This is one area where much greater control is required than for hardware design. In order to develop the software design, the various communicating processes have to be brought together. This bringing together is where interface, or communication, control is paramount. With formal design review meetings these interfaces should be identified in the minutes of meetings and actions can be monitored through to close out.

It is the 'informal' review meetings which are more difficult to audit. By an 'informal' review is meant a meeting held spontaneously between two, possibly three, software design engineers to discuss applications and interfaces. Experience has shown that generally, in such instances, no minutes are kept and sometimes important conclusions are reached. It is, therefore , imperative that all personnel involved in software design keep 'action logs' which notate the actions they take and identify decisions made. These action logs are auditable documents.

An action log would normally comprise a book or day by day diary. It requires considerable self-discipline to maintain an action log but such can become an invaluable document should problems subsequently arise.

Design interface control

There could be situations in the design of computer software where more than one design contractor is utilised or where part of the design is subcontracted. The methods of interfacing, together with interface areas, should be clearly defined.

Again, this activity is executed and controlled in the same manner as for hardware design.

Change control

In software parlance, this is generally known as configuration control. Many organisations have great problems in this area, yet if changes are controlled in a formalised manner, the problems should be few.

Experience has shown that generally too many personnel are allowed access to design information stored in computers and these same people have the ability to amend or modify a design. During such a modification exercise, little thought is given to the impact that such a modification may have on other disciplines and a simple act of making what is thought to be a minor modification could present enormous problems later on.

Design changes or modifications should be agreed by all involved disciplines before the software is amended. The changes should be documented, as for engineering design control, and the necessary approval for the change to be implemented should be obtained. Access into the computer program to undertake changes should be strictly controlled by utilising confidential entry codes. It is considered prudent to limit this access to possibly two people and these people should make changes only with the signed approval of designated responsible personnel.

Access to view the design could, of course, be made available to personnel on the 'need to know' basis.

There could be a facility within the software system for changes or modifications to be stored and, say once a week, reviewed by the appropriate personnel to consider their implications and to authorise implementation as necessary. This storage system should be independent of the main software program.

Whatever method is used, either hard copy or software storage, details of changes or modifications should be retained on file, in order that there is the objective evidence of the change in the event of subsequent problems. This leaves what is generally known as an audit trail.

External design reviews
These are, once again, the same as for engineering design.

Audit and corrective action
All in all, the bases for auditing computer software design activities are straightforward, provided the documentary evidence of quality is maintained by all concerned. The production of a quality plan should be, therefore, a fundamental requirement.

This has been just a brief look into computer software control and further reading on the subject is referenced in the bibliography.

In order to complete the total presentation, the role of quality circles should now be considered.

17

The role of quality circles

Quality circles can play a very important role within the total presentation of quality assurance and it is to be emphasised that circles are a part and only a part of a total quality assurance scheme. Circles should not be considered an end in themselves but more in the nature of a means to an end.

Many organisations believe, or have been led to believe, that by implementating quality circles all quality problems would be solved. Naturally, such organisations become very disillusioned when it is discovered that such is not the case. The implementation of circles as an end in themselves could be likened in such cases to installing a central heating system and then leaving the windows wide open.

WHAT ARE QUALITY CIRCLES?

Quality circles are groups of four to twelve people who perform similar roles and who come from the same work area. These people meet voluntarily on a regular basis to identify and analyse problems and to establish solutions to the problems. The solutions are then presented to management for evaluation and approval. The circle is then often responsible for implementation and effectiveness of the solution.

The quality circle operates in a similar fashion to the quality assurance auditor, whereby a deficiency (problem) is identified, corrective action is taken to correct the deficiency and action taken to prevent recurrence. As for any form of corrective action there must be management involvement if action is to be effective.

Quality circles relate directly to the quality of the product and/or service and, as with the quality control activity, there is no direct involvement in activities which occurred previously. What is more, a single quality circle would deal only with problems or subjects related specifically to its own area of operation, although some solutions may affect other work areas.

It should not be assumed, however, that quality circles will work only in a manufacturing environment. Any organisation where numbers of people are engaged in similar activities can utilise the circle philosophies. Indeed, many financial and business organisations have successfully implemented circles as part of their overall quality strategy.

It should neither be assumed that quality circles are formed to discuss only product- or service-related problems.

As the circle members will be experts in their own particular function, their knowledge and experience should be utilised to suggest ways of increasing job satisfaction, which should, in turn, enhance the quality of their working life.

In the preface to this book reference was made to Yamanouchi san as having been instrumental in the author's understanding of the Japanese approach, not only with regard to the quality of the product but also regarding the quality of life—private life as well as working life. Both affect each other.

Yamanouchi san was, at one time, a circle leader and his particular circle did put forward to management many suggestions to improve the product and many suggestions which made the operators' tasks simpler and more effective. Most of these suggestions were accepted by management for implementation and, where they were not accepted, the management went to great lengths to discuss their reasoning with the circle members. This attitude, in turn, enhanced operator satisfaction, particularly as the operators themselves felt they had a contribution to make and were, so to speak, masters of their own destiny.

The Japanese are considered to be experts in quality circles applications, and, because of their success in this direction, many Western organisations are led to believe that circles are a Japanese invention. This is not entirely the case. Circles certainly developed in Japan following the introduction, from the USA, of statistical quality control methods during the 1950s.

The Japanese success has received international acclaim and Western industries are now looking towards achieving similar successes. The author, having worked in Japan for many years, has been able to understand, to a certain extent, the Japanese way of thinking and consequently is convinced that, because of the wide differences between Western and Japanese culture, the West may not achieve the same success in circle implementation. This, however, should not deter Western industry from adopting circle philosophies as indeed any success, however small, must be considered worthwhile, providing implementation costs do not exceed the beneficial results.

THE COMPANY-WIDE APPROACH

Any philosophy which enhances the quality of the product or service should be implemented on a company-wide basis. As for the total presentation *Gesamtkunstwerk,* quality circles could be considered as one of the arts in the total art work and would, therefore require direction. This direction must be by senior management and, as has been said many times before, the commitment must come from senior management.

FIRST CONSIDERATIONS

Before embarking on a circle programme, therefore, many things should be taken into consideration, such as:

Reasons for introducing a quality circle programme.
Associated costs.
Methods of establishing the circles programme.
Education of management and the work-force in the understanding of, and the benefits to be derived from, such a programme.
Employee acceptance.
Training
Organisational structure for circles.
Implementation.
Methods of evaluating effectiveness.

Taking each of thes considerations in turn:

Reasons for introducing a quality circle programme

An organisation should understand that a quality circle programme can produce effective results but it should not be treated as an end to product-related problems. The programme should be considered as company-wide and not just an isolated technique which can be switched off and on as effectiveness rises or falls.

Quality circles are introduced for many reasons and the most generally accepted are for improvements in:

The quality of the product or service.
Employee satisfaction.
Communication.
Employee effectiveness.
Company competitiveness.

It is, therefore, up to each individual organisation to establish firmly the reasons before implementing the programme and the reasoning should be made known to the work-force if quality circles are to achieve any success at all. It is, therefore, extremely important that the work-force, together with union representatives, are consulted before any action is taken.

The reasons 'why' are important, as has already been established.

Associated costs

Circles are voluntary participation activities but members meet in company-paid time. Salary and wages costs should, therefore, be taken into account.

There could be a requirement to employ a consultant to assist in, or even undertake, the development of the circle programme.

Costs associated with training of personnel in the application of circles, together with training materials, can be substantial. In some instances, the role of the circles' facilitator, whose responsibilities are described later, could be a full-time occupation.

All these costs should be weighed against the expected savings.

Methods of establishing the circles programme

The methods adopted when setting up and developing the appropriate quality assurance programme (Chapter 4) are, in many instances, equally applicable here.

A working party should be established, and the responsibility for the formation of this should lie with a senior member of staff who has knowledge of the activities or functions which are recognised as likely to receive the most benefit from the introduction of circles. This person is given the title 'facilitator'. In general, facilitators can come from any area but experience has shown that most come from one of three areas: production departments, training departments or quality control departments.

It stands to reason that whoever is appointed to the facilitator position should be totally committed to circle philosphies if the programme is to have any success. It is an important position and that person could well have similar attributes to that of the quality assurance manager and, indeed, there is a very good argument for such an appointment to be made from within the quality assurance group (providing, of course, the organisation concerned is operating to the quality assurance philosophies put forward in this book).

In addition to the facilitator, the steering committee should include representatives of management, quality assurance, trade unions and/or other employee spokesmen.

A circle leader is usually chosen from the supervisory staff to whom, in normal everyday circumstances, the circle members would report. This, however, does not preclude others from the responsibility, providing there is evidence of suitable training and experience to support such an appointment.

The working party, once established, would then:

(1) Determine the requirements for third party (consultancy) assistance in developing the programme, training the participants and the eventual implementation of the scheme.
(2) Define responsibilities and lines of communication between individual circles through to management.
(3) Communicate to all employees the reasons for, and the benefits to be derived from, the implementation of quality circles.

Education of the workforce

It is recommended that this be carried out by third party sources—a consultant. Again, experience has shown that, by utilising the capabilities of someone outside the organisation, much more credence is given to the subject. The utilisation of third party sources leads to a much greater employee acceptance (the prophet from another land).

Training

Quality circles will never be effective if the work-force is just formed into a collection of groups and told to get on with it. Training in many areas should be given and these areas would include:

Statistical and quality control techniques
Problem-solving
Leadership skills
Brainstorming sessions
Presentation techniques

The requirement for statistical and quality control techniques is particularly important in production-related circles and is essential where mass production is concerned.

Once a problem has been identified then, of course, the techniques of solving such problems do not come automatically—they should be taught.

The skills of leadership, as for management, do require training and experience.

Brainstorming sessions have been found invaluable in problem-solving but the leader of the session should have had the necessary training to evaluate the results effectively.

Presentation techniques are fundamental to quality circles. The circle leader and his team should have the ability to put forward to management, both orally and by means of visual aids, what the problem is, how it was identified and the suggested methods of solving the problem. The suggested methods must be supported by evidence and by proper costing to substantiate the recommendation. A solution to a problem could go unheeded because of inadequate preparation and poor presentation.

In general, most facilitators receive training from third party sources. The facilitators, in turn, are normally responsible for circle leader training, with the circle members receiving training from the facilitator, the circle leader or a combination of both.

Organisational structure for circles

The organisational structure for quality circles has already been touched upon but it is worthwhile looking at in a little more detail.

As has already been said, quality circles are voluntary participation activities—they are for the members. It is well known that, in most organisations where there are successful circle programmes, the circle members become so identified with their respective circles that they give their circle a club atmosphere by giving it a name such as 'The Cubs', 'The Inner Circle', 'The Family Circle' and so on. One particular circle, whose members worked in very hot conditions, named their circle 'The Devil's Disciples'—rather apt, and a very efficient circle which was instrumental in improving working conditions as well as product quality.

The circle objectives are to identify problems, develop solutions and then present the complete case to management for consideration in the hope of approval and implementation. The philosophy of quality circles has been called 'management from the bottom upwards'.

Management is, in effect, delegating some of its responsibilities to the work-force. This should, therefore, relieve management of some of the mundane but time-consuming and important tasks, thus giving more time to the solving of company policy issues.

Another advantage of such a form of delegation is that it leads to a better and more open form of communication, which can, in turn, lead only to an enhancement in employee–management relationships.

The organisation should therefore start with the members themselves. Membership should be strictly voluntary with no enforced membership. Conversely, no one should be banned from membership.

Each circle should appoint a leader and it is usual for this leader to be a supervisor in normal everyday circumstances.

Circles, to be effective, should liaise with each other, so that related problems can be discussed. There is, therefore, the need for a co-ordinator—the co-ordinator is the facilitator already referred to. The facilitator provides the link not only between individual circles but also between the circles and management. As such, the facilitator will be instrumental in overseeing the development of the circle programme and assisting with, and co-ordinating, the circle meetings. This person will also watch over circle activities with regard to problem identification and solving and eventual implementation of solutions. Obtaining the necessary funding for the circle programme will also be within the realm of the facilitator.

In some large organisations where circle programmes are identified for several locations with two or more facilitators, there would be a requirement for an upper structure co-ordinator to bring it all together. A 'senior facilitator' perhaps!

The circle leaders are primarily responsible for the effectiveness of the meetings and should ensure that all circle members are adequately trained in problem-solving techniques.

Implementation
Areas or activities which can benefit from quality circle participation are areas where people work together and experience similar problems. Typically:

  Accounts
  Administration
  Design/Engineering
  Production

Each circle within any of these areas should set itself a project. Initially, until circle members are practised in problem-solving, the projects should be small in nature. It is a well-known fact that the smaller problems, which can be quickly solved and which are generally overlooked by management, can have a much greater impact upon the well-being of the work-force and the company as a whole than the solutions to major problems which involve considerable expenditure in cost, time and resources and affect only a small part of the business with limited beneficial results.

Some examples of activities for circle consideration are:

Repair/reworking of rejected items
Scrap reduction
Maintenance
Productivity improvements
Design changes
Document control
Invoicing

A schedule should be developed for circle meetings. Invariably the type of project chosen will dictate the frequency of meetings. On average these will probably be once a week at a predetermined time. The length of the meeting should be limited and experience has shown that one hour is usually adequate. A well 'chaired' meeting of one hour can usually achieve far more than a two-hour free for all. Hence the need for a well-trained leader; otherwise the circle might degenerate into a time-wasting talking shop.

A systematic approach should be made to problem-solving. The causes should be investigated and solutions discussed and tested. Documentary evidence should be developed to support the anticipated effectiveness of the proposed solution.

Circle leaders should consider also whether the project will have an effect on other circles. In such cases there could be a need to invite the other 'affected' circle's leader to the meeting.

Problems can, in many instances, be solved quicker if experts or specialists are invited. For example, the project under review may relate to welding; it would be prudent therefore to invite someone from the matallurgical department to give some expert advice.

Methods of evaluating effectiveness

The methods of evaluating effectiveness can be many and varied. A lot will depend on the nature of the project.

Production-related problems, which have been 'solved' by circle members, could result in tangible savings in areas such as:

Reduction in scrap
Reduction in repairs/reworking
Speed-up in unit assembly

In the main, experience has shown that the benefits resulting from the introduction of quality circle programmes are:

Improvements in quality and efficiency
Improvements in communication and co-operation

Improvements in management–employee relationships
Enhanced job satisfaction

Improvements in quality and efficiency can be measured in monetary terms provided management is aware of quality costs.

Improvements in communication and co-operation are difficult to measure in monetary terms but their effect can be seen in the improvements in management–employee relationship.

Enhanced job satisfaction should lead to a greater feeling of 'belonging' and should result in a reduction of absenteeism with increased efficiency.

CONCLUSION

The implementation of a quality circle programme should be given great consideration, particularly in the circumstances previously discussed.

The UK National Society for Quality Circles gives the following essential factors for success (reprinted with the kind permission of the NSQC from its publication *Circle Programme Guidelines*):

Voluntary participation
Members and leaders must be volunteers.

Top management support
The most senior manager of the unit must be committed to the programme—making it clear by example that all the management team are expected to give their active support.

Operational management support
Management must be seen to be interested by committing the employee time for regular circle meetings, attending circle meetings when invited and helping with the implementation of approved solutions.

Facilitator guidance
At least one suitable individual must be able to devote sufficient time to the circle programme. This activity can be combined with other duties, but a programme of around 15 circles is likely to be a full-time job.

Training
Facilitators, leaders and members must be properly trained in team-work, in problem-solving and in presentation skills. At the beginning of a programme, at least the facilitator (and often the first leaders) are trained by a consultant or other professionally competent resource. The facilitator can subsequently train leaders and help them in turn to train their circle members.

Shared work background
Circles should initially be formed from people from the same work area. Shared work knowledge helps a faster development of the essential team-work and also helps the circle to contain problems to those under its

members' direct control.

Solution orientated

Circles must work in a systematic way on solving problems—not just discussing them—investigating causes, testing solutions and whenever possible being involved in the implementation.

Recognition

Circles are not paid directly for their solutions but management should arrange for recognition by means of visits or special events, or by contributions to social functions.

A quality circle programme will not solve all problems. Management should also get its own house in order. Circles, where they can be implemented, should be only a part of a company's quality assurance programme—an integral part where no activity is subservient to the other. Each activity—administration, sales, marketing, finance, design, procurement, manufacture, installation, maintenance, after-sales service, and so on—are all a part of *Gesamtkunstwerk*: the total presentation. This total presentation could be summed up in 8 C's:

Commitment
Co-operation
Communication
Capability   Customer=Competitiveness
Credibility
Confidence

Any form of quality assurance/management system will work only if it has the *commitment* of management and the *co-operation* of all concerned. To co-operate one must *communicate*. Thus comes the *capability* in the work we do which must give *credibility* and *confidence*, not only to the senior executive but to the most important person of all—the *customer*. If customers are happy then this must enhance *competitiveness*.

18

Future trends

The principles and practices of the total presentation described in this book are ideal. As was established in the early pages, any quality programme should be developed to suit the individual workings of an organisation. What has been written in these pages can be used only as a foundation on which to build quality systems.

MASTER THE THEORY BEFORE BREAKING THE RULES!

The author is reminded in this instance, when studying composition of music, of his introduction to harmony. It was instilled into him that the theory of harmony harboured certain fundamental rules with regard to harmonic progression, such as the avoidance of consecutive thirds, fifths and octaves; the leading note should always rise to the tonic; the end of a phrase always marked by a certain harmonic formula, and many, many others.

Having learnt the theory and practised it true to its rules, one was then given licence to break the rules to suit musical taste and application. The same could be said of the contents of this book. Here is the theory which has been found to work well in practice. The 'rules' could well be broken to suit individual company needs. Take what is required and adapt to suit!

In general, it is the high-technology industries that have taken the lead in adopting these principles of quality assurance and not unnaturally expect and demand their suppliers to employ the same principles. The requirement has, therefore, been imposed upon the supplier by the buyer rather than the supplier recognising for himself the need for the implementation of a company-wide policy of total application, which could, and would, be 'good for him'. This is unfortunate. If a home-based high-technology company cannot obtain the materiel it requires, to an appropriate specification and to proper quality standards from a home-based supplier, it will look elsewhere. As many industries know to their cost, this has happened all too frequently.

WHICH DIRECTION?

Industry, in general, is slowly beginning to realise the benefits of quality assurance as discussed in this book. Its importance is increasingly recognised at government level as many governments have introduced schemes for its promotion. A number of trends may be mentioned:

First, the national schemes which many countries are adopting which take the form of financial assistance to enable a company to obtain the services of a management consultant. Such schemes are admirable and many companies are benefiting from them. Unfortunately, such schemes necessarily rely on the abilities of the consultants who are involved and abilities of consultants are rather like the 'curate's egg'—good in parts.

Secondly, reciprocal product certification schemes are being developed. These schemes serve to assess the product and to verify compatibility with mutually agreed standards. Such schemes can lead only to a greater interchange of marketing between the countries involved in them and must inevitably lead to a wider variety of choice to the benefit of the customer. As has already been said, certification confirms that a product meets certain minimum requirements laid down in a standard or statutory documents; what it does not reveal, however, are the problems encountered in getting the product certified. Well thought out quality systems, implemented with management support and commitment, will lead to the reduction and eventually the total elimination of such problems. Certification and quality systems should go hand in hand.

Thirdly, government imposition of quality systems upon contractors is now the rule in certain industries in some countries. This is coercion rather than persuasion but if it takes legislation to make industry realise the potential of an effective quality assurance programme, then perhaps one should not object to its imposition, although force is not necessarily effective. 'He that complies against his will is of his own opinion still' (Samuel Butler, 1613–1680, *Hudibras III*: 3: 547).

Fourthly, training in quality assurance/management systems applications is now beginning to make some headway. Many engineering, scientific and business degree courses are including quality assurance concepts but there is still a long way to go in this respect. Unfortunately, many of the engineering disciplines still seem to view quality assurance as a new name for inspection and testing and have yet to realise its significance in its total management aspects.

Degree courses in quality-related subjects have been in vogue in the USA for some years and the benefits of such education are now beginning to be realised in many other countries. Universities and colleges are beginning to take note and are developing suitable courses.

The fact still remains that, regardless of the type of 'quality' education, in general the students are from 'quality' departments. It is the exception rather than the rule to see a senior executive at a seminar or training course, which leads one to believe that senior executives still normally feel that they can delegate their quality responsibilities, which they most certainly cannot. The commitment must come from the top if all are to get it right first time, every time.

Finally, an effective quality assurance programme, as has been shown, can lead only to increased productivity, efficiency, higher profitability and increased competitiveness.

Appendix A. Standards associated with quality assurance

(Although all titles are given in English, it should not be assumed that the related document is published in the English language.)

GENERAL STANDARDS

Australia

AS 1821—1975	Quality Control System—Level 1
AS 1822—1975	Quality Control System—Level 2
AS 1823—1975	Quality Control System—Level 3
AS 2000—1978	Guide to AS 1821–23
	Suppliers Quality Control Systems

Published by the Standard Association of Australia*

Canada

CSA.Z299.0—1979	Guide for Selecting and Implementing the CSA.Z299 Quality Program Standard
CSA.Z299.1—1978	Quality Assurance Program Requirements
CSA.Z299.2—1979	Quality Control Program Requirements
CSA.Z299.3—1979	Quality Verification Program Requirements
CSA.Z299.4—1979	Inspection Program Requirements
CAN.3–Q395–81	Quality Audits

Published by the Canadian Standards Association†

France

NF.L06–150:1983	Quality assurance and management
	Technical inspection and operators qualification marks

---

* Australian Standards 1821–23 revised November 1985.

† Canadian Standard Z299 revised August 1985. Now titled:
    CAN3-Z299.1-85 — Category 1
    CAN3-Z299.2-85 — Category 2
    CAN3-Z299.3.85 — Category 3
    CAN3-Z299.4-85 — Category 4.

NF.X50–104:1974 Advanced quality assurance programme
NF.X50–110:1980 Recommendations for a system of quality management for use by companies
NF.X50–111:1982 Guide for the selection of quality assurance measures
NF.X50–112:1983 Quality audits in customer/supplier relationships
Published by Association Française de Normalisation (French Standards Association)

International
ISO/DP 9000 (Draft proposal)   Guide to Quality Management and Quality Assurance Standards
ISO/DIS 9001 (Draft Standard)   Quality Systems: Assurance of Design/Development, Production, Installation and Servicing Capability
ISO/DIS 9002 (Draft Standard)   Quality Systems: Assurance of Production and Installation Capability
ISO/DIS 9003 (Draft Standard)   Quality Systems: Assurance of Final Inspection and Test Capability
ISO/DP 9004 (Draft proposal)   Guide to Quality Management Elements
To be published by the International Organisation for Standardisation

Germany (West)
DIN.55.350   Concepts in quality assurance and statistics
Draft 1983   Concepts in quality assurance
    Concepts in quality (assurance) systems
Published by Deutsches Institut für Normung (German Standards Institute)

Hungary
MI.18783:1979   Quality assurance
MI.18798/2:1982   Quality costs. Analysis and use of data
MI.18827:1983   Conditions of establishing quality assurance systems in enterprises
Published by Magyar Népköztársasági Országos Szabvány (Hungarian Office for Standardisation)

India
ISI.10201:1982   Manual on quality assurance systems
Published by the Indian Standards Institution

Ireland
IS.300:Part 0 1984   Quality System Management
IS.300:Part 1 1984   Quality System Requirements—Demonstration of Design, Development, Production and Installation Capability
IS.300:Part 2 1984   Quality System Requirements—Demonstration of Production and Installation Capability

IS.300:Part 3 1984   Quality System Requirements—Demonstration of
                       Final Inspection and Test Capability
Published by the Institute for Industrial Research and Standards

Netherlands

NPR.2645:1980   Explanatory notes to the standards NEN.2646, 2647
                 and 2648 concerning quality assurance

NEN.2646:1980   Quality assurance. General conditions for quality sys-
                 tems for designing, manufacturing and delivery of
                 products and services and for the application of
                 processes

NEN.2647:1980   Quality assurance. General conditions for quality sys-
                 tems for manufacturing and delivery of products and
                 services of which the design is already established
                 and for the application of processes

NEN.2648:1980   Quality assurance. General conditions for quality sys-
                 tems for inspection and delivery of final products or
                 final services

NEN.2650:1981   Guide to the implementation, within an organisation,
                 of a quality system complying with the conditions
                 of the standards on quality assurance NEN.2646,
                 2647 or 2648

Published by Nederlands Normalisatie-Instituut (Netherlands Standards
Institute)

Norway

NS.5801:1981   Requirements for the contractor's quality
                     assurance—Quality assurance system
NS.5802:1981   Requirements for the contractor's quality
                     assurance—Inspection system
NS.5803:1981   Requirements for the contractor's quality
                     assurance—Basic inspection
NVS.Information 16 1984   Guidelines for the interpretation and use of
                         NS.5801

Published by Norsk Verkstedsindustris Standardiseringssentral (Norwegian
Engineering Industries Standardisation Centre)

South Africa

SABS.0157
Parts I–III:1978   Code of practice for quality management systems
   Part 1   Quality system for design, manufacture and installation
   Part 2   Quality system for manufacture and installation
   Part 3   Quality system for final inspection
Published by South African Bureau of Standards

Switzerland
SN.029100:1982   Requirements for quality assurance systems
Published by Schweizerische Normen-Vereinigung (Swiss Association for Standardisation)

United Kingdom
BS.4778:1979   Glossary of terms used in quality assurance (including reliability and maintainability terms)
BS.4891:1972   A guide to quality assurance
BS.5750   Quality systems
  Part 1:1979   Specification for design, manufacture and installation
  Part 2:1979   Specification for manufacture and installation
  Part 3:1979   Specification for final inspection and test
  Part 4:1981   Guide to use of BS.5750 Part 1
  Part 5:1981   Guide to use of BS.5750 Part 2
  Part 6:1981   Guide to use of BS.5750 Part 3
Published by British Standards Institution

USA
ANSI/ASQC:Z-1.15 1979   Generic guidelines for quality systems
Published by American Society for Quality Control

INDUSTRY-RELATED STANDARDS

Nuclear
Canada
CAN3–N2860.82
Published by Canadian Standards Association

International
ISO.6215:1980   Nuclear power plants: Quality Assurance
Published by International Organisation for Standardisation

United Kingdom
BS.5882:1980   Specification for a Total quality assurance programme for nuclear power plants
Published by British Standards Institution

USA
ANSI/ASME.NQA-1 1983   Quality Assurance Program Requirements for Nuclear Facilities
ANSI/ASME.NQA-2 1983   Quality Assurance Requirements for Nuclear Power Plants
Published by American Society of Mechanical Engineers

Military

International

AQAP-1   NATO Quality Control System Requirements for Industry
AQAP-4   NATO Inspection System Requirements for Industry
AQAP-9   NATO Basic Inspection Requirements for Industry
Published by Allied Quality Assurance Publications

United Kingdom

DEF STAN 05-21/1   Quality Control System Requirements for Industry
DEF STAN 05-24/1   Inspection Requirements for Industry
DEF STAN 05-29/1   Basic Inspection Requirements for Industry
Published by Her Majesty's Stationery Office

USA

MIL-Q-9858A   Quality Program Requirements
Published by US Military.

Bibliography

QUALITY ASSURANCE AND MANAGEMENT SYSTEMS

Burgess, J. A. (1984) *Design assurance for engineers,* New York: Marcel Dekker Inc.

Crosby, P. B. (1979) *Quality is free,* New York: McGraw-Hill Book Company.

Crosby, P. B. (1984) *Quality without tears,* New York: McGraw-Hill Book Company.

Deming, W. (1982) *Quality, productivity and competitive position.* Massachusetts: Institute of Technology.

Department of Trade and Industry (1983) *The case for quality,* London: Her Majesty's Stationery Office.

Department of Trade and Industry (1983) *Quality management: A guide for chief executives,* London: Her Majesty's Stationery Office.

Dunn, R., and Ullman, R. (1982) *Quality assurance for computer software,* New York: McGraw-Hill Book Company.

Feigenbaum, A. V. (1983) *Total quality control,* 3rd edition, New York: McGraw-Hill Book Company.

Hayes, G. E. (1983) *Quality assurance: Management and technology,*

Johnson, L. M. (1982) *Quality assurance program evaluation,* Santa Fe Springs: Stockton Trade Press.

Juran, J. M. (1964) *Managerial breakthrough,* New York: McGraw-Hill Book Company.

Juran, J. M. and Gryna, F. M. (1980) *Quality planning and analysis,* New York: McGraw-Hill Book Company.

Peters, T. J., and Waterman, R. H. (1982) *In search of excellence,* New York: Harper and Row.

Roberts, G. W. (1983) *Quality assurance in research and development,* New York: Marcel Dekker Inc.

Sayle, A. J. (1981) *Management audits,* London: McGraw-Hill Book Company.

QUALITY CIRCLES

Barra, R. (1983) *Putting quality circles to work,* New York: McGraw-Hill Book Company.

Department of Trade and Industry (1985) *Quality circles,* London: Her Majesty's Stationery Office.

Hutchins, D. (1985) *The quality circle handbook,* London: Pitman Publishing Limited.

Mohr, W., and Mohr, H. (1983) *Quality circles: Changing images of people at work,* Reading, Mass.: Addison Wesley.

NSQC (1985) *Circle programme guidelines,* London: National Society of Quality Circles.

Robson, M. (1982) *Quality circles: A practical guide,* Aldershot: Gower Publishing Company.

QUALITY CONTROL AND STATISTICS

Caplen, R. H. (1983) *A practical approach to quality control,* 4th edition, London: Business Books Limited.

Cochran, W. G. (1977) *Sampling techniques.* 3rd edition.

Dodge, H. F., and Romig, H. G. (1959) *Sampling inspection tables: Single and double sampling.*

Grant E. L., and Leavenworth, R. S. (1980) *Statistical quality control,* 5th edition, New York: McGraw-Hill Book Company.

Ishikawa, K. (1982) *Guide to quality control,* 2nd revised English edition, Tokyo: Asian Productivity Organisation.

Juran, J. M., Gryna, F. M., and Bingham, R. S. (1979) *Quality control handbook,* 3rd edition, New York: McGraw-Hill Book Company.

Price, F. (1984) *Right first time,* Aldershot: Gower Publishing Company.

Shapiro, S. S., and Gross, A. J. (1981) *Statistical modeling techniques.*

Schilling, E. S. (1982) *Acceptance sampling in quality control,* New York: Marcel Dekker Inc.

Index

Page numbers in italic type refer to the formal definitions of terms.